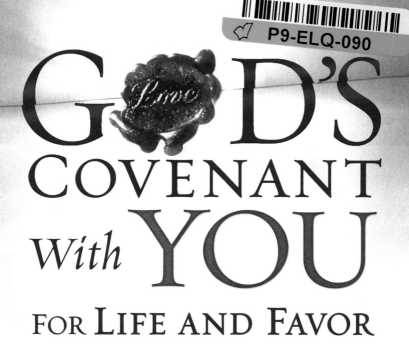

GOD'S COVENANT

With YOU

FOR LIFE AND FAVOR

JOHN ECKHARDT

CHARISMA
HOUSE

Most CHARISMA HOUSE BOOK GROUP products are available at special quantity discounts for bulk purchase for sales promotions, premiums, fund-raising, and educational needs. For details, write Charisma House Book Group, 600 Rinehart Road, Lake Mary, Florida 32746, or telephone (407) 333-0600.

GOD'S COVENANT WITH YOU FOR LIFE AND FAVOR
    by John Eckhardt
Published by Charisma House
Charisma Media/Charisma House Book Group
600 Rinehart Road
Lake Mary, Florida 32746
www.charismahouse.com

Cover design by Justin Evans

Visit the author's website at www.johneckhardtministries.com.

Library of Congress Cataloging-in-Publication Data:
An application to register this book for cataloging has been submitted to the Library of Congress.

International Standard Book Number: 978-1-62998-014-0
E-book ISBN: 978-1-62998-015-7

First edition

15 16 17 18 19 — 987654321
Printed in the United States of America

CONTENTS

CHAPTER 1

COVENANT WITH GOD GUARANTEES LIFE AND FAVOR

[Covenant is] probably the least understood, yet most important concept in the entire Bible. It is at once the heart and the foundation of mankind's relationship with God.[1]

—J. E. LEONARD

THE IDEA OF living a good life full of success, blessing, and favor can be controversial among the people of God. Some want to be blessed and live abundantly but feel guilty about it. Others feel that believers should not want wealth. They believe that when we get saved we should all take a vow of poverty. The other extreme is seeing God as a slot machine. They think, "If I get the right formula for prayer, praise, faith, and declaration, I'll get my blessing."

Living a successful life is more than money. We need to expand our understanding of prosperity. According to *Strong's Complete Concordance of the Bible*, one Hebrew word for prosperity is *shalom*, which is the word for peace. *Shalom* is also "completeness, soundness, welfare, *and* peace." It represents completeness in number and safety and soundness in your physical body. *Shalom* also covers relationships with God and with people.

Prosperity is quietness, ease, abundance, and peace. Words associated with *ease* are goodness, agreeable, benefit, welfare, prosperity, and happiness.

There is an all-encompassing nature to peace that covers every area of our lives. If we are in financial distress, can't find or keep a job, have recurring difficulties in our relationships, and are never able to realize our dreams, we are not at peace.

Christ brings peace into our lives through covenant. God's covenant with us is a covenant of peace. Living a good and prosperous

1

life has everything to do with dwelling in the covenant of peace or shalom with God. Religion has conditioned us to believe that life should be full of trouble and that one day by and by we will go to heaven and then we will have peace. Peace is not only for heaven but also for the here and now on the earth. Your days should not be full of trouble. That doesn't mean trouble will not come, but you can stand up and tell trouble to go. You do not have to live a life of worry and anxiety. Peace is yours. Prosperity is yours. Even when trouble comes, it will not take away your peace.

The whole world is looking for peace. But there is only one way to peace, and that is through Jesus. He says, "I am the way..." (John 14:6). In Judges 6:24 He is called Jehovah Shalom: "The-LORD-Is-Peace." Jesus is part of the Trinity. Whomever They are identified as, Jesus is too. Having Jesus in your heart is the way of peace. No Jesus; no peace. That's when prosperity comes; that is when blessing comes. Peace is what you have as a saint of God.

You are also a peacemaker, and according to Matthew 5:9, you are blessed. You bring shalom wherever you go because Jesus is inside of you. You can change the whole atmosphere of a room because the Prince of Peace lives inside of you. This is your covenant.

> How beautiful are the feet of those who preach the
> gospel of peace, who bring glad tidings of good things!
> —ROMANS 10:15

The gospel is that Jesus Christ came and died so that you could experience the shalom of God. The chastisement—the price—of our peace was upon Him. He was beaten and crucified so we could have peace. All who believe and come under the rule of the Messiah can have peace.

You can have prosperity and live in safety, and all the evil beasts will be driven from your life. You will not be tormented by devils. You will have the blessing of God. It's the guarantee of His covenant of peace. It belongs to the saints of God. So no matter how bad the news gets, don't let the devil take your peace and your shalom away from you.

No matter what goes on, say, "Jehovah Shalom, You are my peace. You are my prosperity. You're the One who gives me shalom. I refuse to be tormented by the devil, to be vexed, harassed, oppressed, poor, or broke. I refuse to not have the peace of God because Jesus was chastised for my peace. I am a saint of God. I am in covenant. I have a right to peace. I can walk in that covenant. A thousand can fall at my side and ten thousand at my right hand, but it will not come nigh me, because I have a covenant of shalom."

Realize that it is not something coming one day. It's here, and it's yours. Jesus is the Prince of Peace. Do you have Jesus on the inside of you? His peace is supernatural. It's already done. All you have to do is walk in faith and it's yours. This is why Jesus came.

KEEPING YOUR PEACE IN A CHAOTIC WORLD

> For the kingdom of God is not eating and drinking, but righteousness and peace and joy in the Holy Spirit.
>
> —ROMANS 14:17

Peace is the kingdom of God. If you're not in the kingdom, you don't have shalom. If you call yourself a child of God, but you keep up a lot of confusion, there's something wrong. A child of God is a peacemaker (Rom. 12:18; Heb. 12:14). Are you a peaceable person? Do you like mess? The church is intended by God to be a model of shalom to the world.

When the world is struggling to find peace, where can they go? Whom can they turn to? Where is the model for peace? Whom can the world look at to see a model for peace? Whom can they look at as a group of people from all different backgrounds—black and white, Jew and Gentile, coming together and living in peace because of the Prince of Peace? There is only one place that this happens—the church, where the wolf lies down with the lamb (Isa. 11:6; 65:25).

This is a picture that represents the coming of the Prince of Peace into the hearts of people whereby they can love people whom they once hated. You can't be a child of God if you hate people. The church is the one place where we can show the world how to live in peace. That's our calling, and for it we will be blessed. Blessed are the shalom makers!

Sometimes we can get so caught up in strife that we begin to think that it's normal to have problems. But it's not. Command good days in your life to be at peace and full of blessing and prosperity. Speak blessing and prosperity over your neighbors, your family members, and your coworkers.

> He who would love life and see good days, let him keep his tongue from evil, and his lips from speaking deceit. Let him turn away from evil and do good; let him seek peace and pursue it.
> —1 Peter 3:10–11, mev

Some don't think they are living unless it's hard. But that is not what Jesus died for you to have. You can have a good life, especially when you refrain your tongue from evil. Watch your mouth. Don't gossip, argue, fight, or add to confusion. And don't keep company with people who take part in that behavior. Seek peace. Peace is prosperity. You cannot have prosperity if you don't control your tongue. A blessed person is someone who knows how to guard his tongue.

The kingdom of God is a community of peace. Saved people are peaceful people. You can disagree with somebody and still be peaceable. Contention does not belong in the house of God—or in the lives of His people. James 3:17 says, "But the wisdom that is from above is first pure, then peaceable, gentle, willing to yield ["easy to be intreated" (kjv), approachable], full of mercy and good fruits, without partiality and without hypocrisy."

When you're walking in God's wisdom, hearing from heaven and hearing the voice of God…when you're getting your wisdom from above, not earthly or fleshly wisdom…when Christ becomes your wisdom, you will go into prosperity. One of the benefits of wisdom is prosperity. Proverbs 3:16 says that riches and honor are in the hands of the wise. The wise and prosperous are peacemakers.

> Blessed (enjoying enviable happiness, spiritually prosperous—with life-joy and satisfaction in God's favor and salvation, regardless of their outward conditions) are the makers and maintainers of peace, for they shall be called the sons of God!
>
> —MATTHEW 5:9, AMP

Prosperous people will walk away from a fight and confusion even if they don't get their point across. They see strife as detrimental to their prosperity. They do not make room for it in their lives. "Follow peace with all men…" (Heb. 12:14, KJV).

Peace is one of the fruit of the Spirit (Gal. 5:22). As a child of God, confusion and strife vex you and don't agree with your spirit. You can't be around that. It is not *normal*. The church is to be God's community of shalom.

> If it is possible, as much as depends on you, live peaceably with all men.
>
> —ROMANS 12:18

Prosperous people are peaceful people. They are blessed. They have more than enough. They love life and see good days. They are citizens of the heavenly kingdom of God because they have been redeemed from the curses of sin and death.

WHAT WILL A COVENANT WITH GOD BRING INTO YOUR LIFE?

> Blessed be the Lord, who daily loadeth us with benefits, even the God of our salvation. Selah.
>
> —PSALM 68:19, KJV

> Bless the LORD, O my soul, and forget not all His benefits.
>
> —PSALM 103:2

> What shall I render unto the LORD for all his benefits
> toward me?
>
> —Psalm 116:12

To bless means "to invoke divine favor on, to bestow happiness, prosperity or good things of all kinds; to make a pronouncement holy; to consecrate, to glorify for the benefits received, to extol for excellencies."[2] Likewise a blessing is "a prayer or solemn wish imploring happiness upon another; a benediction or blessing; the act of pronouncing a benediction or blessing; that which promotes prosperity and welfare."[3] Then in the Hebrew language, "to bless" is the word *barak*, which means "to kneel by implication to bless God as an act of adoration, to praise, salute, thanks...a posture of reverence."[4] And again the word *blessing* in Hebrew is *berakah*, which is "a benediction (an act of invoking a blessing)."[5]

The Lord, through His covenant, wants to shower His blessing and benefits on you. Here are some of the ways He will do it.

- The covenant of peace means your children are taught of the Lord. Claim this for your children and your descendants (Isa. 54:13).
- Your family members who are far off will experience the peace of God. God's peace will come to the nations. The families of the earth will experience the peace of God (Isa. 57:19).
- God's peace will flow into your life like a river. God's presence (sanctuary) will manifest in your life. God's presence brings peace. God multiplies us. Multiplication is a symbol of God's blessing (Ezek. 37:26).
- Christ is our peace (shalom). The new covenant is based on the finished work of Christ. When salvation (Christ) comes into your life, the blessing of peace (shalom) comes (Eph. 2:14).
- The Lord will prosper you. He delights in your prosperity. In other words, God *wants* you (His servant) to prosper (Ps. 35:27; 122:17; 147:14).

As I mentioned briefly, the word *shalom* is also translated "prosperity." God prospers His people. Our covenant gives us the right to enjoy the peace and prosperity of the kingdom. Settle for nothing less than shalom. Thus is your covenant right. Claim it and walk in it today. There is no end to the increase of peace (shalom).

+ God's covenant of peace brings healing and restoration (Isa. 57:19).
+ God's covenant will bring not only peace but also an abundance of peace to your life (Ps. 37:11).
+ God's covenant will cause you to flourish (Ps. 72:7).
+ God's covenant will bring joy, peace, and singing (Isa. 55:12).
+ God's covenant will release His mercy upon your life (Deut. 7:9; Neh. 1:5; 9:32; Ps. 25:10; 89:3, 28; 106:45).
+ God's covenant will release to you His faithfulness, loyalty, and steadfastness (Deut. 7:9; Ps. 118:1, 5–6; 1 Cor. 1:9).

God is the faithful God. Faithfulness is a mark of covenant. God is always faithful to His people and His promises.

God was always faithful to Israel in spite of their unfaithfulness. God kept His covenant with Abraham and brought forth His seed (Jesus) to bless the nations. God was faithful to Israel and sent Jesus to them first to bless them. God was faithful to the house of David and caused David's son to sit on his throne. The Lord will endure forever with His covenant people.

According to *Webster's Dictionary*, the word *steadfast* means, "firmly fixed in place, immovable, not subject to change." The word *endure* means: "to continue, to last, to remain firm under suffering or misfortune without yielding." The word *forever* means, "for a limitless time, at all times, continually, eternally." Hence, the meaning of each of these key words speaks to us of the powerful, firm, trustworthy, tenacious, never-ending love of God.

WHY YOU NEED TO UNDERSTAND COVENANT

Every believer needs a revelation of the benefits of coming into covenant with God. Understanding covenant is important because all of the blessings of salvation are based on covenant. God works through covenant, and we receive based on His covenants. Faithfulness is the most important part of keeping covenant. It is impossible for God to lie and break covenant. When a believer understands God's faithfulness to covenant, he can trust His Word and His promises.

Every covenant has benefits and blessings. The reason why people enter into covenant is because of the benefits derived. There are many benefits of covenant that can be summarized with the word *salvation*. Salvation means more than going to heaven one day. Salvation is deliverance, healing, restoration, protection, freedom, and blessing. God's salvation comes through covenant, and a believer needs to understand the many benefits of salvation.

People in covenant have a special relationship with one another, and in our case it is a covenant with God. God becomes our covenant God, and there are multiple benefits within this relationship that those outside of covenant don't have access to. Whatever the covenant partner has is at your disposal if needed. This includes His power, authority, love, mercy, and protection.

In the next chapter I will discuss how to come into covenant with God for those who have not accepted the full measure of salvation and to reaffirm those who have.

PRAYERS FOR A BLESSED LIFE

Lord, bless me and keep me. Make Your face to shine upon me, and be gracious unto me. Lord, lift up Your countenance upon me and give me peace (Num. 6:24–26).

Make me as Ephraim and Manasseh (Gen. 48:20).

Let me be satisfied with favor and filled with Your blessing (Deut. 33:23).

Lord, command Your blessing upon my life.

Give me revelation, and let me be blessed (Matt. 16:17).

I am the seed of Abraham through Jesus Christ, and I receive the blessing of Abraham. Lord, in blessing, bless me, and in multiplying, multiply me as the stars of heaven and as the sand of the seashore.

Let Your showers of blessing be upon my life (Ezek. 34:26).

Turn every curse sent my way into a blessing (Neh. 13:2).

Let Your blessing make me rich (Prov. 10:22).

Let all nations call me blessed (Mal. 3:12).

Let all generations call me blessed (Luke 1:48).

I am a son of the blessed (Mark 14:61).

I live in the kingdom of the blessed (Mark 11:10).

My sins are forgiven, and I am blessed (Rom. 4:7).

Lord, You daily load me with benefits (Ps. 68:19).

I am chosen by God, and I am blessed (Ps. 65:4).

My seed is blessed (Ps. 37:26).

Let me inherit the land (Ps. 37:22).

I am a part of a holy nation, and I am blessed (Ps. 33:12).

Lord, bless my latter end more than my beginning (Job 42:12).

Lord, let Your presence bless my life (2 Sam. 6:11).

I drink the cup of blessing (1 Cor. 10:16).

Lord, bless me, and cause Your face to shine upon me, that Your way may be known upon the earth and Your saving health among all nations. Let my land yield increase, and let the ends of the earth fear You (Ps. 67).

I know You favor me because my enemies do not triumph over me (Ps. 41:11).

PRAYERS FOR ENLARGEMENT AND INCREASE

Break off of my life any limitations and restrictions placed on my life by any evil spirits in the name of Jesus.

I bind and cast out all python and constrictor spirits in the name of Jesus.

Bless me indeed, and enlarge my coast. Let Your hand be with me, and keep me from evil (1 Chron. 4:10).

Cast out my enemies, and enlarge my borders (Exod. 34:24).

Lord, You have promised to enlarge my borders (Deut. 12:20).

Enlarge my heart so I can run the way of Your commandments (Ps. 119:32).

My mouth is enlarged over my enemies (1 Sam. 2:1).

Enlarge my steps so I can receive Your wealth and prosperity (Isa. 60:5–9).

I receive deliverance and enlargement for my life (Esther 4:14).

The Lord shall increase me more and more, me and my children (Ps. 115:14).

Let Your kingdom and government increase in my life (Isa. 9:7).

Let me increase in the knowledge of God (Col. 2:19).

O Lord, bless me and increase me (Isa. 51:2).

Let me increase exceedingly (Gen. 30:43).

Let me increase with the increase of God (Col. 2:19).

Let me increase and abound in love (1 Thess. 3:12).

Increase my greatness, and comfort me on every side (Ps. 71:21).

Let me increase in wisdom and stature (Luke 2:52).

Let me increase in strength and confound the adversaries (Acts 9:22).

Let Your grace and favor increase in my life.

Let the years of my life be increased (Prov. 9:11).

Let the Word of God increase in my life (Acts 6:7). Bless me in all my increase (Deut. 14:22).

Let my giving and tithes increase (Deut. 14:22).

Let my latter end greatly increase (Job 8:7).

Let me grow in grace and in the knowledge of Jesus Christ (2 Pet. 3:18).

I will flourish like a palm tree and grow like a cedar in Lebanon (Ps. 92:12).

Let my faith grow exceedingly (2 Thess. 1:3).

The breaker is gone up before me and broken through every limitation and barrier of the enemy (Mic. 2:13).

Lord, You are the God of the breakthrough. You have broken forth against my enemies (2 Sam. 5:20).

My branches run over every wall erected by the enemy (Gen. 49:22).

I can run through a troop and leap over a wall (Ps. 18:29).

Let my line go through all the earth, and my words to the end of the world (Ps. 19:4).

I am a joint heir with Jesus Christ. Give me the heathen for my inheritance and the uttermost part of the earth for my possession (Ps. 2:8).

CHAPTER 2
COMING INTO COVENANT WITH GOD

This cup is the new covenant in My blood, which is shed for you.

—LUKE 22:20

THE BIBLE IS a covenantal book that reveals a covenantal God. God's loyalty and faithfulness to covenant is one of the major themes of Scripture. God cannot break covenant. God is faithful and loyal to His people.

We can trust and rely on God's covenant because He is committed to His promises. When God could swear by no higher He swore by Himself.

> For when God made promise to Abraham, because he could swear by no greater, he sware by himself.
>
> —HEBREWS 6:13, KJV

This means we can absolutely trust, rely upon, and depend upon our covenant with God.

A biblical covenant is an agreement—generally between God and man. The stipulations of such an agreement command absolute loyalty as indicated in the first commandment: "You shall have no other gods before Me" (Exod. 20:3; Deut. 5:7).

Covenant (01285) (berit/berith/beriyth) means treaty, compact, agreement between two parties (first used in God's covenant with Noah—Genesis 6:18; 9:9–17). As discussed more below *beriyth* describes a compact made by passing between pieces of flesh. Covenant is a solemn, binding arrangement between two parties and entails a variety of responsibilities, benefits, and penalties depending on the specific covenant.

God enters into covenant with men. This is a very humbling and sobering truth. The fact that the Great God would enter into relationship with men through covenant is amazing. God's purposes are always done through covenant. God's covenant with Abraham was for the purpose of bringing salvation and blessing to the nations. God's covenant with Israel was also for this purpose: to bring the Messiah into the world.

Only One Way to True Peace

In Isaiah 54 God promised His people a covenant of peace (shalom): "For the mountains shall depart, and the hills be removed; but my kindness shall not depart from thee, neither shall the covenant of my peace be removed, saith the Lord that hath mercy on thee" (Isa. 54:10, kjv). But Israel never walked in that covenant of peace consistently because they continued to violate it. The greatest period of shalom was under King Solomon whose name actually means peace. He was the most prosperous king of Israel. For a forty-year period Israel lived under that promise of shalom. But then Solomon married other wives and took part in idolatry, and there was a breech or a split from the covenant God had established.

Peace and shalom come from God. Only He can give it, and He can take it away. We also have the choice to be blessed by walking in covenant with Him or deactivate it by not walking in covenant with Him.

> I form the light, and create darkness: I make peace, and create evil: I the Lord do all these things.
> —Isaiah 45:7, kjv

When you leave God and break His covenant, God will withdraw His shalom and He will allow disaster. The enemy will come into your land and destroy you. The sword will come in the land and prosperity will be destroyed. We see that this is true based on the Israelites experience all through the Book of Judges. But God will send warning and correction. He began to send prophets or "covenant messengers" to a covenant people to warn them of their covenant violation to give them a chance to repent before God's covenant wrath would come upon them. The prophets repeatedly said that there is no peace to the wicked.

If a prophet tells you that you will have a life of peace and you are violating God's Word—His covenant—the prophet is lying, because you will not experience shalom or peace or prosperity if you are not living in covenant with God. When someone is wicked and unrighteous they are not at peace. Do not be fooled.

God promised Israel that if they keep His commandments He would give them that shalom. But they did not listen. However, God had a plan that would not only restore Israel, if they chose, but His plan would also extend to all mankind.

In Jeremiah 31:31–34 God told the people that they would not be able to experience His peace under the old covenant because they continued to break it. He was alluding to the fact that they would only be able to experience God's true peace by way of the Messiah. The Messiah would come to make a new covenant. He came preaching the good news of the kingdom.

The only way you can experience the true shalom of God is through His Son—"Prince of Peace" (Isa. 9:6). Jesus came preaching the "gospel of peace" (Rom. 10:15; Eph. 6:15)—or the gospel of shalom, the gospel of the kingdom. So we have to repent and receive the gospel of peace.

You are under a new covenant when you have accepted Christ's sacrifice for you and submit your life under His authority. But when you reject Christ and His sacrifice, you reject His new covenant and the very shalom you are looking for—like the children of Israel rejected Him when He came. In Luke 19:41–42 Jesus cried over Jerusalem because He knew that if they rejected Him they would not experience shalom but instead experience the sword. He knew that the enemy would build a trench around them and would besiege them on every side and not one stone would be left one upon another. War, famine, poverty, pestilence, and death was coming.

When you reject Jesus, you reject your only hope for peace and prosperity.

Jesus Is Our Covenant

By Jesus coming to earth and bringing salvation and deliverance, we see the personification of God's faithfulness. From the time of Abraham, Isaac, and Jacob, through Moses, David, and the prophets, God had promised to send a deliverer. His name was Jesus, "for He will save His people from their sins" (Matt. 1:21).

That is why in the Gospels we see people approach Jesus with their issues, saying, "Son of David, have mercy upon me." They understood that when the Messiah—the Son of David—came, He would extend God's mercy to Israel and save them from all of their troubles. We see that in the prophecy of Zacharias, father of John the Baptist, found in Luke 1:67–75 (emphasis added):

> Blessed is the Lord God of Israel, for He has visited and redeemed His people, and has raised up a horn of salvation for us in the house of His servant David, as He spoke by the mouth of His holy prophets, who have been since the world began, that we [Israel] should be saved from our enemies and from the hand of all who hate us, *to perform the mercy promised to our fathers and to remember His holy covenant,* the oath which He swore to our father Abraham: to grant us that we, being delivered from the hand of our enemies, might serve Him without fear, in holiness and righteousness before Him all the days of our life.

Here Zacharias was declaring that the Messiah has come and Israel would see through Jesus the greatest manifestation of God's faithfulness and mercy ever known to man—salvation. His incarnation was the manifestation of eternal salvation and eternal redemption. So not only would He perform miracles for Israel, but He would also ensure their eternal redemption, salvation, forgiveness, and bring them into the kingdom.

SALVATION COMES TO THE GENTILES
THROUGH THE NEW COVENANT

Contrary to what we may realize, Jesus was not a minister to everyone. His primary purpose was to fulfill God's covenant promises made to Abraham and to Israel, to confirm them, to fulfill them, to extend mercy to Israel, and to save the remnant. Jeremiah 31:31–34 says:

> I will make a new covenant with the house of Israel and with the house of Judah—not according to the covenant that I made with their fathers in the day that I took them by the hand to lead them out of the land of Egypt, My covenant which they broke, though I was a husband to them, says the LORD. But this is the covenant that I will make with the house of Israel after those days, says the LORD: I will put My law in their minds, and write it on their hearts; and I will be their God, and they shall be My people. No more shall every man teach his neighbor, and every man his brother, saying, "Know the LORD," for they all shall know Me, from the least of them to the greatest of them, says the LORD. For I will forgive their iniquity, and their sin I will remember no more.

He did not come to minister to Jews *and* Gentiles. When Gentiles came to Him for ministry, He was shocked at their faith.

We see this proven in the story of the Gentile woman who came to Jesus and asked Him to heal her daughter. Jesus said, "I was not sent except to the lost sheep of the house of Israel....It is not good to take the children's bread and throw it to the little dogs" (Matt. 15:24–26). That does not seem like a very compassionate or merciful response, to call someone a dog. She persisted and said, "Yes, Lord, yet even the little dogs eat the crumbs which fall from their masters' table" (v. 27). Basically she was saying, "I don't want what belongs to the people of God. I just want what they don't want." Understand that God could have healed and delivered everybody in Israel, but

Israel wasn't taking all that God had. So there were some crumbs available. Crumbs are what's left over. And because Israel left behind so much of what God had for them, Jesus healed her daughter.

People may not understand why Jesus responded to her the way He did. You have to remember that she was a Gentile and was not in covenant with God. She had no right to claim mercy. She had no covenant, no relationship with God. Mercy is connected to covenant. When you are in covenant with God, you can receive mercy. Mercy is available to you.

Let's take a look at another story in Luke 17:12–18:

> Then as He entered a certain village, there met Him ten men who were lepers, who stood afar off. And they lifted up their voices and said, "Jesus, Master, have mercy on us!" So when He saw them, He said to them, "Go, show yourselves to the priests." And so it was that as they went, they were cleansed. And one of them, when he saw that he was healed, returned, and with a loud voice glorified God, and fell down on his face at His feet, giving Him thanks. And he was a Samaritan. So Jesus answered and said, "Were there not ten cleansed? But where are the nine? Were there not any found who returned to give glory to God except this foreigner?"

I believe that this story of the one Samaritan leper who came back is in the Bible to show that Israel received so much mercy from God, but they didn't appreciate it. The Samaritan (a Gentile) was thankful. The outsiders are more thankful than the insiders. The insiders take it for granted. The Samaritan came back and thanked Jesus. He was glad to get healed. He understood that he wasn't a Jew, that he wasn't in covenant, but he still got healed. The other nine went on their merry way. Many of those who are in covenant are often not thankful for the mercy of God. They take it for granted.

Only the remnant of the house of Israel received Jesus's ministry and His fulfillment of the covenant. The rest of Israel hardened their hearts. So God extended His mercy to the Gentiles. That's us! We will get saved. We will get healed. We will get delivered. It was always God's plan that His mercy would go to the nations or the Gentiles. Romans 15:8–9: "Now I say that Jesus Christ has become a servant to the circumcision [to the Jews] for the truth of God, to confirm the promises made to the fathers [Abraham, Jacob, and Isaac], and that the Gentiles might glorify God for His mercy." But remember mercy is connected to covenant. In order for the Gentiles to receive the mercy of God, God had to make a new covenant.

On Passover night Jesus sat down with His disciples and took the bread and the cup and said, "This cup is the new covenant in My blood, which is shed for you" (Luke 22:20). He made a new covenant with those twelve men, the new Israel of God. Now through the death of Christ we all come into a new covenant with God. So all those who were saved in Israel were saved through this new covenant. Then the Gentiles tapped into the covenant and began to receive mercy. Because you have a covenant through the blood of Jesus and you are a believer, mercy is extended to you!

PRAYERS TO ACTIVATE GOD'S COVENANT IN YOUR LIFE

Shalom, prosperity, and peace are mine through Jesus Christ.

I am a saint of God.

I am a child of God.

I have a covenant with God.

My covenant is a covenant of peace, prosperity, and blessing.

I walk in covenant all the days of my life.

I enjoy shalom, prosperity, peace, and safety all the days of my life.

I will walk in covenant.

I will be faithful to the covenant through the blood of Jesus.

I have a covenant of shalom, peace, and prosperity, in my life.

Lord, You keep covenant and mercy with those who love You and keep Your commandments (Exod. 20).

Lord, You bless those who obey Your voice and keep Your covenant.

Lord, I take hold of Your covenant through Your death and sacrifice. I choose life (blessing) (Deut. 30:19).

Let Your blessings come upon me and overtake me (Deut. 28:2).

Let me be blessed in the city and blessed in the field (Deut. 28:3).

Let the fruit of my body be blessed, and let all the fruit of my labor be blessed (Deut. 28:4).

Let my basket and store be blessed (Deut. 28:5, KJV).

Let me be blessed coming in and blessed going out (Deut. 28:6).

Let the enemies of my soul flee before me seven ways (Deut. 28:7).

Command Your blessing upon my storehouses and all I set my hand to, and bless my land (Deut. 28:8).

Establish me as a holy person unto You, Lord (Deut. 28:9).

Let all people see that I am called by Your name (Deut. 28:10).

Make me plenteous in goods (Deut. 28:11).

Open unto me Your good treasure, and let heaven's rain fall upon my life and bless the work of my hand (Deut. 28:12).

Let me lend (give) unto many nations and not borrow (Deut. 28:12).

_____

Make me the head and not the tail (Deut. 28:13).

_____

Let me be above only and not beneath (Deut. 28:13).

_____

CHAPTER 3

TAPPING INTO THE FAVOR OF GOD

*Thou hast granted me life and favour, and thy
visitation hath preserved my spirit.*

—JOB 10:12, KJV

W HAT A BLESSING to be granted life and favor! The Lord does bless His people with life and favor. Life and favor are both gifts from God. This is because He is gracious. He is the Lord, the Lord God, merciful and gracious (Exod. 34:6). Favor is given to those who are in covenant with God, and gives us the extra measure to achieve success while doing the things God has called us to do.

Favor means "grace"; "that which affords joy, pleasure, delight, sweetness, charm, loveliness"; and "good will, benefit, bounty, reward."[1] If you look up the Hebrew and Greek definitions of *prosperity*, many of these words carry over into favor as well.

Favor is goodwill. This is God's kindness and benevolence given to those who love Him. Favor will release great blessings, including: prosperity, health, opportunity, and advancement. The Bible records numerous examples of God's favor upon His people causing them to experience many breakthroughs. Favor is God loving-kindness. I want you to get the full revelation of all that God's covenant of peace can mean for you.

God's peace (shalom)—favor, grace, loving-kindness, blessing, goodness, joy, prosperity, health, opportunity, and advancement— can come upon your life. God desires to bring the fullness of His shalom to you.

Further definitions of favor include "preferential treatment," "to be partial to," "to make easier," "to support," "to perform a kindness for," "favoritism; good will; liking."

22

Synonyms for favor include prefer, like, approve, endorse, support, lean toward, honor, be partial to; grant favors to, further, promote, treat with partiality, show consideration for, make an exception for, treat as a special character, use one's influence for, treat as a special character.

This is what God will do for you. You can live life with divine assistance and intervention. You can enjoy "favored child" status. There are tremendous benefits that come with the favor of God. In order to enjoy these benefits, you must learn how to tap into the favor of God.

LEVELS OF FAVOR

Before I share with you how to tap into the favor of God, I want you to know that you already have favor with God. If you are saved, you are in covenant with God and therefore you have received favor. Your salvation is a favor from God. There are, however, different levels of favor. You can increase in favor.

> Jesus increased in wisdom and stature, and in favour with God and man.
>
> —LUKE 2:52, KJV

Jesus increased in favor with God and man. You can also increase in favor with God and man. You should not remain at the same level of favor. There are greater realms of favor available for you to walk in.

> Great grace was upon them all.
>
> —ACTS 4:33

Grace, as I described previously, is the same as favor. It is the Greek word *charis*, which means favor.[2] Wherever you see the word *grace* you can think of favor. The church in the Book of Acts had great grace (favor). There is favor and then there is *great* favor. We want to enter into the realm of great favor.

> ...much more they which receive abundance of grace and
> the gift of righteousness shall reign in life by one, Jesus
> Christ.
>
> —Romans 5:17, kjv

There is an abundance of grace (favor). Those who receive an abundance of favor will reign in life by Jesus Christ. We want to be able to enter into the realm of abundance of favor. God is a God of abundance. He is able to do exceeding abundantly above all that we ask or think (Eph. 3:20).

> Grace and peace be multiplied unto you through the
> knowledge of God, and of Jesus our Lord.
>
> —2 Peter 1:2, kjv

Favor can be multiplied. You can receive an abundance of grace by having it multiplied unto you. You can increase in grace through multiplication. We want to enter into the realm of favor where favor is multiplied unto us.

Don't limit the amount of favor you can walk in. God's favor is limitless. We should continue to increase in favor. The more favor you receive and walk in, the more miracles and breakthroughs you will see. You will have more open doors. You will see more financial miracles.

There will be a generation of believers who will walk in more favor than any previous generation. God is releasing an abundance of grace (favor) upon the earth. It is time for the church to receive and walk in this abundance.

This generation will walk in levels of favor that others have never walked in. Get ready to receive and walk in levels of favor you have never experienced before!

> Let not mercy and truth forsake thee: bind them about
> thy neck; write them upon the table of thine heart: So
> shalt thou find favour and good understanding in the
> sight of God and man.
>
> —Proverbs 3:3–4, kjv

MERCY AND COMPASSION INCREASE
THE FAVOR OF GOD

There are ways to increase the favor of God in your life. One way is to walk in mercy and truth. *Mercy* is the Hebrew word *checed*, which means kindness or pity. It also means favor. In other words as you show favor to others, you will reap favor. This is simply the law of sowing and reaping. As you are kind to others showing them pity and mercy, you will receive favor. To pity means to show compassion. This is being concerned about and helping others.

Selfish people don't walk in favor. Hardness of heart will stop the flow of God's favor. Because iniquity will abound, the love of many will wax cold (Matt. 24:12). You cannot afford to shut up your bowels of compassion and expect to walk in God's favor (1 John 3:17).

> He is gracious [charismatic], and full of compassion [merciful], and righteous [just]. A good man sheweth favour and lendeth....He hath dispersed [scattered], he hath given to the poor [needy]...
> —PSALM 112:4–5, 9, KJV

This is the kind of man who walks in the favor of the Lord. He sows favor and reaps favor. Favor is multiplied unto him through the law of sowing and reaping. He has pity upon the poor and gives. He is merciful and compassionate. God favors those who favor others.

FAITHFULNESS INCREASES THE FAVOR OF GOD

Truth is the Hebrew word *emeth*, meaning stability, certainty, and trustworthiness. To be trustworthy means to be reliable. Are you a reliable person? Can people count on you to do what you say? Is your word your bond? These are the questions you need to ask yourself. If you want favor with God and man you must be trustworthy. You must be faithful. To be faithful means to be worthy of trust or belief.

> Now God had brought Daniel into favour and tender love with the prince of the eunuchs.
> —DANIEL 1:9, KJV

O Daniel, a man greatly beloved.
—DANIEL 10:11

Then the presidents and princes sought to find occasion against Daniel concerning the kingdom; but they could find none occasion, nor fault; forasmuch as he was faithful [trustworthy].
—DANIEL 6:4, KJV

Daniel was a man who walked in God's favor. He had favor with God and man. He was greatly beloved. Notice that he was also a faithful man. This was a key to Daniel receiving so much favor.

And Joseph found grace [favor] in his sight.
—GENESIS 39:4, KJV

The same was true of Joseph. He was trustworthy. He would not sin with his master's wife because he was faithful. He knew that his master trusted him with everything in his house. He did not sin with Potiphar's wife although she pressed him daily.

If you have not been trustworthy, then repent and begin to keep your word. Become faithful to the house of God. Become a faithful employee. Get to work on time. Be trustworthy on the job. Be trustworthy in all your relationships. Be faithful to your spouse. The favor of God will being to flow into your life. Make the necessary changes and watch God's favor begin to flow.

Operate in mercy and truth. Heal the sick. Cast out devils. Feed the hungry. Clothe the naked. These are all mercy ministries.

Preach the truth. Teach the truth. Don't compromise when it comes to the Word of God. God's Word is truth (John 17:17). Be a doer of the Word! Stand on the Word! Defend the truth!

Be truthful. Don't lie. Don't live a hypocritical lifestyle. These things will cut the flow of favor from your life. Don't follow false teaching. Stay with the truth. Follow sound doctrine.

Live a life that is honest before God and man (2 Cor. 8:21). Honesty will cause God's favor to come upon you. God loves honesty. Honesty is truthfulness and sincerity.

> Grace [favor] be with all them that love the Lord Jesus
> Christ in sincerity. Amen.
>
> —EPHESIANS 6:24, KJV

Favor is released to those who are sincere in their walk with God. Sincere means genuine with no hypocrisy or pretense. Are you sincere in your walk with God? If the answer is yes, then expect favor to come into your life.

GENEROSITY INCREASES FAVOR

Giving is another way to tap into the favor of God. "A good man sheweth favour, and lendeth" (Ps. 112:5, KJV). Giving is one of the ways you show favor to others. There is one type of giving I want to emphasize that will cause favor to be multiplied to you in ways you may have never experienced. There is a realm of favor that this type of giving will bring you into that no other type of giving will.

> And God is able to make all grace [favor] abound toward
> you [superabound]; that ye, always having all sufficiency
> in all things, may abound to every good work: (As it is
> written, He hath *dispersed abroad*; he hath given to the
> poor: his righteousness remaineth for ever....)
>
> —2 CORINTHIANS 9:8–9, KJV, EMPHASIS ADDED

I have emphasized "dispersed abroad." Years ago the Lord challenged our ministry to begin to sow into other nations. He wanted us to disperse abroad. There is an abundance of favor that is released to a ministry that disperses abroad. God will make favor "superabound" toward you. This is the literal meaning of the word *abound* in the Greek language. There will come a superabundance of favor.

Most believers have never walked in this level of favor. It is available to those who will disperse abroad. Showing mercy and giving to poor nations is the way to tap into this realm of favor.

There will be an abundance of financial favor released to them who disperse abroad. God will multiply your seed sown. This is how you can enter into the realm of multiplication. Multiplication always brings an abundance.

Stinginess will choke the flow of favor out of your life. You cannot be stingy and have an abundance of favor. Givers receive favor. "Give and it shall be given unto you, good measure, pressed down, shaken together, and running over [overflowing], shall men give into your bosom" (Luke 6:38, KJV). Men will favor you by giving into your bosom. There will be so much favor until your finances will overflow. This is an abundance of favor. We want to walk and live in the level of "abundance of favor."

GREAT GRACE (FAVOR)

> And with great power the apostles gave witness to the resurrection of the Lord Jesus. And great grace [favor] was upon them all.
>
> —ACTS 4:33

Great is the Greek word *megas*. We get the word *mega* from this word. In other words, they had mega-grace. Mega means large. It also means "a million." There are megabucks, megabytes, megadoses, and megahertz. The implication is always something huge. We want to enter into the realm of mega-favor.

The apostles' anointing releases great favor. This is a part of the apostolic church. There is no lack when there is this level of favor.

> I thank my God always on your behalf, for the grace [favor] of God which is given you by Jesus Christ; that in everything ye are enriched by him, in all utterance, and in all knowledge; even as the testimony of Christ was confirmed in you: So that ye come behind in no gift; waiting for the coming of our Lord Jesus Christ.
>
> —1 CORINTHIANS 1:4–7, KJV

This is great favor. When you walk in this realm of favor, you will come behind in no gift. You will be enriched in everything. *To enrich* means to make rich. *To be rich* means to have an abundant supply. This is a level of favor that releases abundance.

The apostles would release grace when writing to the churches. This is a part of apostolic ministry. There is an anointing upon apostles and other ministry gifts to release favor to the body of Christ. Favor and apostleship are linked together (Rom. 1:5).

As their churches become more apostolic, they will increase in favor. This is the hour in which God is restoring apostolic ministry to the church. The church is again receiving the ministry of the apostle. Apostles are once again being recognized. As true apostles minister, we will see a great release of God's favor to the church. This is already happening. It is the time of God's favor. This is the year of the Lord's favor.

> Thou shalt arise, and have mercy upon Zion: for the time
> to favour her, yea, the set time, is come.
>
> —PSALM 102:13, KJV

We are living in apostolic time. This is a season of favor. God is doing some awesome things in this season. He is working a work so great that it will not be believed (Hab. 1:5). It is a set time. This means that it has been ordained of the Father. No devil can stop it. You must believe it and receive God's favor.

FAVOR MULTIPLIED THROUGH KNOWLEDGE, WISDOM, AND UNDERSTANDING

> Grace [favor] and peace be multiplied unto you through
> the knowledge of God, and of Jesus our Lord.
>
> —2 PETER 1:2, KJV

Favor is multiplied through the knowledge of God and of Jesus our Lord. This means that as we increase in the knowledge of God and the Lord Jesus, we increase in favor. This is how favor is multiplied—through knowledge. I always encourage the saints to study. Read good books. Learn more about the things of God. Increase in wisdom. Associate with wise people. When you increase in wisdom, you will also increase in favor.

> For whoso findeth me findeth life, and shall obtain favour of the Lord.
>
> —Proverbs 8:35, kjv

This is wisdom speaking. Wisdom releases favor. We need wisdom. It is the principle thing. We need wisdom, knowledge, and understanding. Good understanding brings favor (Prov. 13:15). We'll talk more about wisdom in the next chapter.

Now let's connect knowledge, wisdom, and understanding to apostolic ministry. Apostles are sent by God to bring revelation to the church (Eph. 3). They help the church to walk in the manifold wisdom of God (Eph. 3:10). God's wisdom is manifold. This means it is multifaceted. God's wisdom covers every aspect of life. It is not limited to just one revelation.

There are many different aspects of God. A knowledge of God means you know Him in His manifold dimensions. You understand the apostolic, prophetic, evangelistic, pastoral, and teaching characteristics of God.

You should understand healing, deliverance, prosperity, faith, love, praise, worship, holiness, and all the other truths that the Holy Spirit is revealing to the church. As you increase in knowledge, favor is multiplied unto you.

Ignorance will stop the flow of favor. Don't remain in ignorance. Study, read, and learn. Listen to good messages. Attend a church where the Word of God is being taught. Associate with people who know God. Knowledge is a spirit (Isa. 11:2). The spirit of knowledge will be imparted unto you as you associate with people who really know God.

We want to get into the realm of favor where it is multiplied. Multiplication brings tremendous increase. To multiply means to increase the amount, number, or degree of. This is God's desire for you. He wants to multiply His favor in your life. When you increase in knowledge, He will multiply His favor unto you.

When favor is multiplied, you will begin to have an abundance of favor, and the work of your hands will be fruitful. You will then be able to reign in life. It takes favor to reign. David was able to reign because of God's favor. He overcame every obstacle because of God's favor.

> For thou art the glory of their strength: and in thy favour our horn shall be exalted.
> —PSALM 89:17, KJV

Favor brings exaltation. It brings promotion and honor.

> ...even the rich among the people shall intreat thy favour.
> —PSALM 45:12, KJV

Ask the Lord for favor. We have not because we ask not. Ask for favor on the job. Ask for favor in your ministry. Ask God for favor over your business and your family relationships. God delights in giving favor. If the rich entreat God's favor, surely the poor can. Ask for God's favor in any area of lack in your life. Favor will change your situation.

Favor will release breakthroughs. Favor will release finances. Favor will release property. Favor will open new doors.

FAVOR COMES TO THE HUMBLE

> But he giveth more grace [favor]. Wherefore he saith, God resisteth the proud, but giveth grace [favor] to the humble.
> —JAMES 4:6, KJV

Favor comes to the humble. Those who recognize their need and ask can receive. Pride will cut the flow of favor from your life.

Humility is necessary to operate in God's favor. As you humble yourself and entreat God's favor, He will grant you more favor. Repeat the confessions at the end of this chapter. Begin to tap into the favor of God through prayer, humility, giving, mercy, truth, and knowledge. Receive and walk in the abundance of favor all the days of your life.

My Testimony of Favor

I was born in Chicago and spent the majority of my early life living in one small block of the city until I got married. I had never moved outside of this small area. I had never been on a plane.

My mother was an Italian Catholic, full-blooded Sicilian. She loved the pope; she loved the Catholic Church. She was Italian. My grandparents were from Sicily. When I say she was Italian and Catholic, I mean when the Pope came to Chicago, my mother cried. She said, "Oh, just look at him…" I had just been saved and I said, "Mama, he isn't any holier than me." She said, almost crying, "Watch your mouth, Johnny! How dare you. He's a holy man. He's given his whole life to God, and here you are just now starting to read the Bible."

My mother was a single parent, and of course she wanted me to go to Catholic school, so somehow she got enough money to send me to Holy Angels Catholic School. I went to Catholic school from kindergarten to eighth grade. I had to wear a uniform with the little cross tie. I remember that they would let us out of school at 3:00 p.m., fifteen minutes before the public schools to give us a head start to get home, because the public school kids were waiting to beat up the little Catholic school kids.

I remember the services at church. They did mass in Latin. It seemed so holy. I didn't know what they were saying, but I figured if I had to sit through it I had to be going to heaven.

In the eighth grade a Catholic priest blessed my life. He came to me and told me that I had been chosen to go to a private high school in the suburbs. The priest told me that a sponsor had come forward and offered to pay my tuition for all four years at Loyola Academy, a private, all-boys school at the time, and one of the top schools in the city, and I didn't have to pay one dime of tuition for four years. I was going to school with "the rich kids." I had to ride the train every day from my small block in the middle of Chicago to go to school in the suburb of Wilmette, Illinois, with kids who lived in neighborhoods entirely different from mine. It is a very expensive school. There was no way I could have afforded it.

I'll never forget: my sponsor was the owner of a large company. I had a chance to spend time in his home. He lived in an affluent neighborhood in a large mansion. I'm from a small little apartment in Chicago, and there I was staying with this man and his family in their mansion. This is the favor of God. I didn't have enough money to go to that kind of school.

Then in my senior year at Loyola Academy, some faculty members came and asked me where I wanted to go to college? I said, "Well, I think I want to go to Northwestern." I didn't realize it was one of the most expensive schools in the Big 10. They said, "OK, we're going to give you a scholarship and pay your way to go to Northwestern." Now, I didn't have a dime in my pocket. I'm from a small block in Chicago. There I was at Loyola Academy, getting ready to go to Northwestern University. I was going to school with people who had money, and I didn't have enough sense to know I wasn't "supposed" to fit in. I didn't have enough sense to be intimidated or think I didn't belong. I had the favor of God on my life and didn't know it.

In my junior year at Northwestern I got saved and began attending Crusaders Church. Now with salvation, the blessing of God really came. When I got saved, I gave my whole heart to God. I plunged into this thing. I was all the way in. I told all my friends good-bye. They thought I was crazy. I wouldn't get high with them anymore. Before that I smoked dope and took acid. I gave all that up when I got saved in 1978.

Since that time the favor of God has increased in my life. God has taken me around the world. I have ministered in seventy nations. I've met prime ministers and presidents. I've been to the White House. None of this was because of me. I am a man who grew up in the hood. So I'm not just talking about something I read about in the Bible. I'm telling you, when the favor of God comes on your life, it will take you places you could not go on your own. You might not have a dime in your pocket, but God says, "Don't worry. You don't need money; you need favor. I'll have somebody pay for it for you."

Another thing: the greatest way I believe that favor can come upon a man is based on the scripture that says, "He who finds a wife finds a good thing, and obtains favor from the Lord" (Prov. 18:22). A good wife is from God's favor. And I have a good wife. She is smart, wise, and loves God. She keeps me straight and tells me when I am about to do something foolish.

And finally, I have a group of people who love me—Crusaders Church. That's favor! I run into pastors all the time who talk about how hard it is, how their members don't treat them right. My members treat me well. They love me. Some of them have been with me twenty or thirty years. Since I haven't run them out by now, I know that's the favor of God.

Listen, I was the first one in my family, among my friends, and in my neighborhood to be saved, and it wasn't because of me. I didn't have enough sense to get saved. Sin makes you a fool. It was the favor of God that called me out of where I was and drew me in.

You Need Favor

The favor of God can change your life. If you are saved today, it is only because of the grace and favor of God. You are not good enough to be saved on your own. God looked over so many others and chose you. God chose you because He loves you. It's not because of who you are or what you've done; it's because of His favor. You are elected by God. Chosen before the foundation of the world. Thank God for the Holy Ghost who drew you.

As I said at the beginning of this chapter, life and favor are gifts of God. We don't need luck. We need blessing. We need favor. We need the blessing of God. God desires to release new favor on your life. When you have God's favor and blessing, there is nothing in life that can hold you down.

When you begin to walk in the favor and blessing of the Lord, others will recognize it. The favor and blessing of God on your life is one of the most powerful things that can be released to you.

Matthew 6:33 says, "Seek ye first the kingdom of God, and his righteousness; and *all* these things shall be added unto you" (KJV, emphasis added).

God says, "You don't need money. You need My favor." You need His shalom—the full measure of peace—to operate in your life. This is your gift from Him if you are His child, if you are in covenant with Him. God blesses His people and rescues them. Just as He did with the Israelites.

In Ezekiel 16:1–14 God talks to the children of Israel about how He found them in a rejected state where they had been thrown away and no one wanted them. They were drowning in their own blood. But when God passed by them, He said to them, "LIVE!" Then He blessed them and adorned them with jewels.

God is saying this same thing to you. Maybe you were thrown away to die and had no chance at living a good life. Maybe no one wanted you or you were not born with a silver spoon in your mouth. But when God looked upon you He had mercy on you.

God will not only save you and wash you, but He will also bless you, dress you up, put jewels on you, and beautify you. The grace and favor of God on your life will cause you to go into a place of prosperity. God not only will save you but will also multiply you and bless you.

PRAYERS THAT RELEASE THE FAVOR OF GOD

Father, I thank You for Your favor. I believe in the power of favor. I humble myself and ask for your favor. I need your favor in every area of my life.

I believe I am increasing in favor. I desire to walk in higher levels of favor. I receive an abundance of favor, and I reign in life through Your favor. I receive great favor.

As I grow in the knowledge of You and the Lord Jesus Christ, I believe favor is multiplied unto me. I am a giver. As I give, Your favor is abounding toward me. I am merciful and trustworthy. I have favor with God and man.

I believe you will support me, endorse me, help me, make things easier for me, promote me, and honor me because of Your favor. I enjoy "favored child" status from my heavenly Father. Your favor surrounds me as a shield. I am sincere in my love of Jesus.

Your favor overflows in my life. Thank You, Father, for Your favor. I praise You and give You glory for Your favor.

Lord, You have granted me life and favor.

Lord, I thank You for life and life more abundantly.

I thank You for favor coming upon my life.

I believe that new life and new favor have been ordained for me.

Today I receive new life and new favor.

I believe favor is a gift of heaven.

I receive the gift of life—the gift of eternal life.

I receive the gift of favor and the gift of grace upon my life in the name of Jesus.

Thank You, Lord, for new grace and new favor, new prosperity and new blessing coming on my life.

I am the apple of God's eye.

I am one of God's favorites.

God favors me, loves me, and has chosen me from the foundation of the world to receive His grace and favor.

I receive extraordinary favor on my life in the name of Jesus!

Let me be well favored (Gen. 39:6).

Lord, show me mercy and give me favor (Gen. 39:21).

Give me favor in the sight of the world (Exod. 12:36).

Let me be satisfied with your favor like Naphtali (Deut. 33:23).

Let me have favor with You, Lord, and with men (1 Sam. 2:26).

Let me have favor with the king (1 Sam. 16:22).

Let me have great favor in the sight of the king (1 Kings 11:19).

Let me find favor like Esther (Esther 2:17).

Thou hast granted me life and favour, and Thy visitation hath preserved my spirit (Job 10:12, KJV).

I pray unto You, Lord, grant me favor (Job 33:26).

Bless me and surround me with favor like a shield (Ps. 5:12).

In Your favor is life (Ps. 30:5).

Make my mountain stand strong by Your favor (Ps. 30:7).

Because of Your favor, the enemy will not triumph over me (Ps. 41:11).

Through Your favor, I am brought back from captivity (Ps. 85:1).

Let my horn be exalted through Your favor (Ps. 89:17).

My set time of favor has come (Ps. 102:13).

I entreat Your favor with my whole heart (Ps. 119:58).

Let Your favor be as a cloud of the latter rain (Prov. 16:15).

Let Your favor be upon my life as the dew upon the grass (Prov. 19:12).

I choose Your loving favor rather than gold and silver (Prov. 22:1).

Let me be highly favored (Luke 1:28)

Show me Your marvelous loving-kindness (Ps. 17:7).

Remember Your mercy and loving-kindness in my life (Ps. 25:6).

Your loving-kindness is before my eyes (Ps. 26:3).

I receive Your excellent loving-kindness (Ps. 36:7).

Continue Your loving-kindness in my life (Ps. 36:10).

Let Your loving-kindness and Your truth continually preserve me (Ps. 40:11).

Command Your loving-kindness in the daytime (Ps. 42:8).

Your loving-kindness is good; turn unto me according to the multitude of Your tender mercies (Ps. 69:16).

Quicken me after Thy loving-kindness (Ps. 119:88, KJV).

Hear my voice according to Your loving-kindness (Ps. 119:149).

You have drawn me with Your loving-kindness (Jer. 32:18).

CHAPTER 4
A LIFE OF EXCELLENCE AND WISDOM

O ye simple, understand wisdom: and, ye fools, be ye of an under-
standing heart. Hear; for I will speak of excellent things; and
the opening of my lips shall be right things. For my mouth shall
speak truth; and wickedness is an abomination to my lips.

—PROVERBS 8:5–7, KJV

XCELLENCE AND WISDOM are pillars in the life of a covenant believer. A life of excellence is a life of wisdom, knowledge, and understanding. Wisdom is excellent. Wisdom is the highest and the principal thing. Wisdom is superior. God is excellent in wisdom. God desires for us to partake of this excellency of wisdom. He says, "Have not I written to thee excellent things in counsels and knowledge?" Wisdom is the better thing, the more excellent thing.

Studying and walking in the Word of God will provide you with a foundation for excellence. God's Word is His wisdom. The fear of the Lord is the beginning of wisdom. The fear of the Lord is a foundation for a life of excellence. We are to approve and prize what is excellent.

> So that you may surely learn to sense what is vital, and approve and prize what is excellent and of real value [recognizing the highest and the best, and distinguishing the moral differences].
> —PHILIPPIANS 1:10, AMP

A life of excellence is pursuing what is excellent, which includes wisdom and love. This is *not* the excellency of worldly wisdom but the excellency of divine wisdom.

39

WISDOM IS PRINCIPAL

> Get wisdom!...Do not forsake her, and she will preserve you; love her, and she will keep you. Wisdom is principal; therefore get wisdom. And with all your getting, get understanding. Exalt her, and she will promote you; she will bring you honor, when you embrace her....When you walk, your steps will not be hindered, and when you run, you will not stumble. Take firm hold of instruction, do not let her go; keep her, for she is your life.
>
> —PROVERBS 4:5–8, 12–13, MEV

Wisdom is the principal thing. Wisdom enables you to live life accordingly. In Proverbs 4 we witness Solomon talking to his son about the supernatural wisdom that was imparted to Him by God. Solomon was acting as the Lord would have fathers to act. Fathers are to impart wisdom to their sons and daughters. In this season we are experiencing the crisis of a fatherless generation. Many men have abdicated their roles as fathers. They are leaving a generation orphaned to fend for themselves and to figure out on their own how to be successful in life.

Many of these same men did not have fathers to impart wisdom to them either. You cannot impart to someone else what you do not carry. But God said He would be a father to the fatherless. He has also set in place surrogate fathers to fill the gap. We just need to ask God for wisdom, and He will teach us through the life, actions, and words of godly leaders—and sometimes by His own direct influence in your life.

He said that if we ask Him for wisdom, He would give it to us liberally, without restraint or limit. James 1:5 says, "If any of you lack wisdom, let him ask of God, who gives to all liberally and without reproach, and it will be given to him." You see, God wants you to have every gift, resource, and tool you need to live the life He has granted you.

Wisdom leads you to make good decisions.

Without wisdom, you will wander through life blind not knowing which way to go or what decision to make to get you where you need to go. A life without wisdom is full of trouble. You can't always blame the devil for your troubles. Sometimes it is a simple as a lack of wisdom. Sometimes the troubles in life are a result of some unwise decision-making.

You will not prosper in life without the ability to make wise decisions. There are some anointed people who know how to prophesy, cast out devils, and shout all over the church, but when it comes to their personal lives, they make bad decisions. Then they say the devil is attacking them. No, the devil wasn't even around. It was their unwise decisions. They may know how to dance, preach, shout, speak in tongues, and prophesy, but they don't pay their rent. Then when the landlord shows up, they think he's the devil. There's no need throwing oil on him; just pay your rent on time. You can't blame the devil for that.

Wisdom will lead you to not only make the right decision at the right time, but it also causes you to own up to your weaknesses and correct them with courage and humility.

With wisdom comes discipline and self-control.

You need discipline to learn that you cannot live your life doing stupid things and be successful. You cannot live a life of excellence without discipline and self-control.

Are there any areas in your life that are out of control? Are you carried away, disorderly, out of hand, rebellious, uncontrollable, ungovernable, unmanageable, unruly, or undisciplined? If the answer is yes, then you are without walls. An undisciplined lifestyle will bring you into bondage and sabotage your opportunities for success in life. There is no lasting deliverance and freedom without discipline.

Proverbs 25:28 says, "He that hath no rule over his own spirit is like a city that is broken down, and without walls" (KJV). Cities without walls were open to invasion and attack from outside forces.

A person without self-control is open for demonic thieves to come in and steal their peace and sabotage their opportunities for success.

In order to experience success, these are the areas over which you need self-control:

+ Thinking—"Finally, brethren, whatsoever things are true, whatsoever things are honest, whatsoever things are just, whatsoever things are pure, whatsoever things are lovely, whatsoever things are of good report; if there be any virtue, and if there be any praise, think on these things" (Phil. 4:8, KJV).

+ Appetite—"And put a knife to thy throat, if thou be a man given to appetite" (Prov. 23:2, KJV).

+ Speech—"As a city open, and without compass of walls; so *is* a man that may not refrain his spirit in speaking" (Prov. 25:28, WYC).

+ Sexual character—"But I keep under my body, and bring it into subjection: lest that by any means, when I have preached to others, I myself should be a castaway" (1 Cor. 9:27, KJV).

+ Emotions—"A merry heart maketh a cheerful countenance: but by sorrow of the heart the spirit is broken" (Prov. 15:13, KJV).

+ Temper—"Be not hasty in thy spirit to be angry: for anger resteth in the bosom of fools" (Eccl. 7:9, KJV).

There are some believers who do not understand the correlation between wisdom, discipline, and success. You cannot sustain the blessing of God in your life if you do not have discipline and self-control.

I've heard of people coming into prayer lines with their seed saying, "I'm believing in God for a sixteen-bedroom mansion." But they can't even take care of an apartment. When you get a bigger house, there are bigger bills and a bigger lawn to cut. So if you can't take care of a closet, pay rent on time, or go into work faithfully every day, then how can you believe that God will give you more? That's not wisdom.

It is wisdom and discipline that prepare you for more in life. You may be able to get to a level of success on your own, but discipline and wisdom will keep you there and set you up for greater things. Proverbs 4:6 and 8 says that wisdom will "preserve you...and she will keep you...and she will promote you."

Wisdom will lead you to right relationships.

> Do not enter the path of the wicked, and do not go in the way of evil men. Avoid it, do not travel on it; turn from it and pass on. For they do not sleep unless they have done mischief; and their sleep is taken away unless they cause some to fall. For they eat the bread of wickedness and drink the wine of violence.
> —Proverbs 4:14–17, mev

Wisdom will tell you, "Get away from idiots." You cannot hang out with foolish people and get ahead in life. You have to choose the right people to partner with. The Bible talks about being unequally yoked with unbelievers (2 Cor. 6:14), and being a believer is more than just a confession; it is a lifestyle. Some people will tell you they are saved, but they live for the devil. Don't be deceived.

Proverbs 4:14–17 is direct advice for who not to be in relationship with if you want to maintain a level of excellence, focus, and success in your life. There are people who God has pinpointed for you to connect with. They actually have some sense. Pray about potential alliances and let the wisdom of the Lord lead you to those relationships that bring peace and harmony into your life.

If this is new revelation to you and the Lord has just spoken some names of individuals who are not right for where you are going in life, you need to let them know that you can't hang out with them anymore. They have no dreams, no vision.

I shared my testimony with you earlier about how I immediately told my friends bye, when I got saved. They were going in a different direction than I was. I wasn't getting high on dope and acid anymore; they were. Those were not relationships I could maintain and still see God's favor in my life. Trust me, I know exactly where I came from, that's why I left.

You have to know how to leave. You need to know when it's time to go. Make wisdom you're companion. She will tell you when it's time to go. She will preserve your life.

> Listen for God's voice in everything you do, everywhere you go; he's the one who will keep you on track.
> —Proverbs 3:5, The Message

Fear of the Lord Brings Wisdom

> The fear of the Lord is the beginning of wisdom, and the knowledge of the Holy One is understanding.
> —Proverbs 9:10, mev

Listening with reverence and awe (fear) to the voice of God over your life and then walking in obedience to what you hear is wisdom. God will not steer you wrong. He has set the boundary lines—His path for you to have abundant life and great favor—out before you. He has set you in a pleasant place (Ps. 16:6). He leads you by still and quiet (peaceful) waters, and restores your soul (Ps. 23:2–3). To fear God means that you are careful to follow His guidance and direction, knowing that you risk your very life if you don't. (See Matthew 10:28.) When you fear God, you are submitted to His ways and trust that He has a good plan for your life (Jer. 29:11).

Moral Excellence (Virtue)

> For this reason make every effort to add virtue to your faith; and to your virtue, knowledge.
> —2 Peter 1:5, mev

Wise people are excellent and virtuous in their walk with God. They seek to live right and have excellent characters. Virtue is moral excellence, excellence of character and integrity. Excellence is a talent or quality, which is unusually good and so surpasses ordinary standards. Excellence represents the highest in standard or quality. Excellence is a key to living an uncommon life. Let's take a look at other translations of 2 Peter 1:5 that confirm the connection between virtue, faith, and excellence.

> This is why you must make every effort to add moral excellence to your faith; and to moral excellence, knowledge.
>
> —CEB

> And for this same reason, and by applying all diligence, supply with your faith excellence of character, and with excellence of character, knowledge.
>
> —LEB

> For this very reason, make every effort to add to your faith excellence, to excellence, knowledge.
>
> —NET

Moral excellence (virtue) is something that is almost lost in society as a goal or standard. There are many Christians who do not add virtue (moral excellence) to their faith. Many believe that excellence is unattainable. It is refreshing to encounter a virtuous person, a person of excellence of character. As Proverbs 31:10 says, "Who can find a virtuous woman? For her worth is far above rubies."

We must be people of excellence if we want to see the favor of God in our lives. We should have a standard of excellence in our character. This should definitely be the standard of leaders. *Excellent* means extraordinary or exceptional. It means to be outstanding. According to Bible.org, "Excellence is a powerful word. It implies something that is obtained by striving; it is an extremely high ideal."[1] Godly success through excellence, diligence, and wisdom is not common in our society of compromise and mediocrity. As people of God, we were made to stand out as lights illuminating the glory of God.

EXCELLENT THINGS

The Lord does excellent things. No one can add or take away from the works of the Lord. Our salvation and redemption are complete (excellent) in Christ. God will do excellent things in your life.

> Sing unto the LORD; for he hath done excellent things:
> this is known in all the earth.
> —ISAIAH 12:5, KJV

Synonyms for excellent include exceptional, magnificent, superlative. Excellence speaks of greatness, completeness, highness, perfection, and the best. God's greatness is excellent and His works are excellent. God's people are called the excellent ones. Do you live up to that name?

> But to the saints that are in the earth, and to the excellent,
> in whom is all my delight.
> —PSALM 16:3, KJV

The excellent ones are the noble ones. *Noble* means having or showing qualities of high moral character, such as courage, generosity, or honor.

God will do excellent things for His excellent ones (the saints). This again speaks of those who are in a covenant relationship with Him. We were made in the image of God, therefore like our Father, we will also do excellent things when we are submitted to Him. Jesus said that we would do greater things than He did.

Believe for excellent things to come to you. Believe that you will do excellent things and see great success in your life. Our God is excellent and will manifest His excellence in your life.

CONSIDER THE ANT

> Go to the ant, thou sluggard; consider her ways, and be
> wise.
> —PROVERBS 6:6, KJV

A wise person is diligent in the right things that lead to life and godliness (2 Pet. 1:3). The ant is a good example of what characterizes this kind of diligence. Ants work tirelessly to gather food in summer for the winter. The ant is the opposite of the sluggard (sloth). The ant does not have an aversion to work. The ant is industrious. *Industrious* means working energetically and devotedly; hard-working; diligent.

+ The ant is persistent, sticking to a job, whether building a nest or gathering food. Do you always stick to a job until it is done and done right?

+ It knows its job and does it, working quietly and without show until the work is done. Do you work without complaining, without whining? Do you do your job quietly?

+ It doesn't need another ant watching to be sure it gets its work done. Can you do a job without someone checking on you to be sure it is being done?

+ It is cooperative, working with others to get big jobs done.[2]

  The incessant and unintermitted activity and diligence with which the ant plies her summer task present another important lesson of wisdom to the rational and accountable family of God. It is not an occasional exercise in which this curious creature is engaged. Day after day do these industrious tribes issue forth to the work of gathering. And here, again, they teach us wisdom.[3]

  —JOHN JOHNSTON

The ant prepares. "The ants are a people not strong, yet they prepare their meat in the summer" (Prov. 30:25, KJV).

The ant is diligent. Diligence is constant and earnest effort to accomplish what is undertaken; persistent exertion of body or mind. Diligence promotes prosperity (riches, plenty) and leads to success.

"He becometh poor that dealeth with a slack hand: but the hand of the diligent maketh rich" (Prov. 10:4, kjv).

> The thoughts of the diligent tend only to plenteousness;
> but of every one that is hasty only to want.
>
> —Proverbs 21:5, kjv

Diligence will put you in a place of authority. Diligence is a key to promotion.

> The hand of the diligent shall bear rule: but the slothful
> shall be under tribute.
>
> —Proverbs 12:24, kjv

> Seest thou a man diligent in his business? he shall stand
> before kings; he shall not stand before mean men.
>
> —Proverbs 22:29, kjv

If you will be wise and diligent like the ant, you will see excellence manifest in your life.

CONFESSIONS FOR WALKING IN WISDOM

I receive the wisdom of God and the fear of the Lord. Let them be a part of my life.

I want to make wise decisions.

I want to know the Word of God.

I believe that wisdom is my companion.

She will bless me.

She will protect me.

She will promote me.

She will exalt me.

Wisdom is the principal thing.

I receive wisdom, the wisdom of the Word, the Spirit of wisdom.

Jesus is my wisdom.

He's in my life.

I receive the wisdom of heaven to walk on the earth.

Thank you, Lord, for blessing me with wisdom.

I will not make foolish decisions.

I will not make foolish choices.

I will not have foolish relationships.

I walk in wisdom all the days of my life, and I am blessed in Jesus's name.

Lord, teach me wisdom's ways and lead me in straight paths (Prov. 4:11).

The Lord's wisdom will save my life (Eccles. 7:12).

I pray for an understanding heart that is enshrined in wisdom (Prov. 14:33).

I tune my ears to Your wisdom, Lord, and concentrate on understanding (Prov. 2:2).

I do not put my trust in human wisdom but in the power of God (1 Cor. 2:5).

In You, O Lord, lie the hidden treasures of wisdom and knowledge (Col. 2:3).

I listen when those who are older speak, for wisdom comes with age (Job 32:7).

Lord, Your wisdom is more profitable than silver, and its wages are better than gold (Prov. 3:14).

Let wisdom multiply my days and add years to my life (Prov. 9:11).

Let my house be built by wisdom and become strong through good sense (Prov. 24:3).

I will not be foolish and trust my own insight, but I will walk in wisdom and be safe (Prov. 28:26).

Let the fruit of my life prove Your wisdom is right (Luke 7:35).

Let the fear of the Lord teach me wisdom (Prov. 15:33).

I will obey Your commands, so that I will grow in wisdom (Ps. 111:10).

Fill me with Your Spirit, O God, and give me great wisdom, ability, and expertise in all kinds of crafts (Exod. 31:3).

Lord, give me wisdom and knowledge to lead effectively (2 Chron. 1:10).

Let those who have gone before me teach me wisdom of old (Job 8:8–10).

True wisdom and power are found in You, God (Job 12:13).

The price of Your wisdom, O Lord, cannot be purchased with jewels mounted in fine gold; its price is far above rubies (Job 28:17–18).

I will keep silent, O God. Teach me wisdom (Job 33:33).

Your wisdom will save me from evil people and from the immoral woman (Prov. 2:12, 16).

I will embrace Your wisdom, for it is happiness and a tree of life to me (Prov. 3:18).

I will pay attention to Your wisdom, O Lord. I will listen carefully to Your wise counsel (Prov. 5:1).

Give me understanding so that Your knowledge and wisdom will come easily to me (Prov. 14:6).

Grant me wisdom so that I may also have good judgment, knowledge, and discernment (Prov. 8:12).

Thank You, Lord, that You will certainly give me the wisdom and knowledge I requested (2 Chron. 1:12).

I will not be impressed with my own wisdom, but I will instead fear the Lord and turn away from evil (Prov. 3:7).

I will not turn my back on Your wisdom, O God, for it will protect and guard me (Prov. 4:6).

Your wisdom is better than strength (Eccles. 9:16).

I thank and praise You, God of my ancestors, for You have given me wisdom and strength (Dan. 2:23).

For You will give me the right words and such wisdom that none of my opponents will be able to reply or refute me (Luke 21:15).

I need wisdom; therefore, I will ask my generous God, and He will give it to me. He will not rebuke me for asking (James 1:5).

I pray that my life pleases You, O God, that You might grant me wisdom, knowledge, and joy (Eccles. 2:26).

CHAPTER 5
MOMENTUM: THE KEY TO SUSTAINING A VICTORIOUS LIFE

David said, "The LORD who delivered me out of the
paw of the lion and out of the paw of the bear, He will
deliver me out of the hand of this Philistine."

—1 SAMUEL 17:37, MEV

COVENANT BELIEVERS ARE victorious believers. Victory is what is obtained after winning a bout with an adversary or opponent. Jesus said that in this world, we would have trouble but to take heart because He has overcome the world (John 16:33). Through Jesus we can have victory over our adversary, the devil.

When we live with an understanding that we have overcome through Jesus, we open ourselves up to living the life He has granted to us through His new covenant. The more we see ourselves overcoming trial after trial and test after test, the more we can believe God for the life He promised. Each victory gives us greater faith for the next test. This is what I call momentum. Momentum is what we need to maintain a life of favor and abundance.

A good example of momentum at work comes from the sports world. Imagine a team that wins few games. Before long this team is on a winning streak. As the team wins more games it picks up momentum. One of the hardest things to do is defeat a team that is on a winning streak. Because the team has momentum it is harder to stop the winning streak. The rule in sports is the team that gets momentum is usually the team that wins.

Political candidates who gain momentum win elections. One issue can give a candidate the momentum needed to win. Armies who get momentum win battles. One strategic advantage can give a person or group the momentum needed to win. The key is to get and maintain momentum.

The Lord desires to give you momentum. It will carry you into realms of the spirit that you will never enter without it. Satan desires to stop your momentum. He knows that if you get momentum, you will have a greater victory, greater success, and greater impact on those around you. You need a revelation of how to get momentum, maintain it, and use it to your advantage as you seek after the life and favor God has promised you.

INCREASING YOUR MOMENTUM

> And Saul said to David, Thou are not able to go against this Philistine to fight with him: for thou are but a youth, and he a man of war from his youth.
>
> And David said unto Saul, Thy servant kept his father's sheep, and there came a lion, and a bear, and took a lamb out of the flock: And I went out after him, and smote him, and delivered it out of his mouth: and when he arose against me, I caught him by his beard, and smote him and slew him. Thy servant slew both the lion and the bear: and this uncircumcised Philistine shall be as one of them, seeing he has defied the armies of the living God.
>
> David said moreover, The LORD that delivered me out of the paw of the lion, and out of the paw of the bear, he will deliver me out of the hand of this Philistine. And Saul said unto David, Go, and the LORD be with thee.
>
> —1 SAMUEL 17:33–37, KJV

One of the keys to getting momentum is to allow your victories to thrust you into greater momentum. David's previous victories gave him the momentum he needed to defeat Goliath. He rehearsed his victories over the lion and the bear before he went into battle against the giant. Each victory the Lord gives you increases your momentum. You should always go into battle with momentum from your previous victories.

Momentum builds your confidence. It increases your strength and skill for the next battle. True champions understand momentum. They know how to get it and maintain it. True leaders also understand the importance of momentum.

Great generals understand its importance on the field battle. They know how to capitalize on their opponent's errors and gain momentum in battle. Once they gain momentum, they know how to use it to defeat their foes. Two of Israel's greatest generals were Joshua and David. They understood the place of momentum in warfare. Both used momentum to destroy their enemies.

Joshua's Momentum

> On the day the Lord gave over the Amorites to the children of Israel, Joshua spoke to the Lord and said in full view of Israel: "Sun, stand still over Gibeon; and moon, in the Valley of Aijalon." So the sun stood still, and the moon stood in place until the people brought vengeance on their enemies. Is this not written in the book of Jashar? The sun stood still in the middle of the sky and did not set for about a full day. There has not been a day like this either before or after it, when the Lord obeyed a man, for the Lord waged war for Israel.
>
> —Joshua 10:12–14, mev

One of the greatest miracles recorded in the Word of God occurred on the field of battle. Joshua spoke and the sun and moon stayed. He received an extra day to defeat his enemies. He understood momentum. Once Joshua saw the enemy's defeat, he would not allow the sun to go down. This miracle gave him the momentum he needed to destroy his enemies. Joshua did not allow darkness to come and stop his momentum. He kept it, by a miracle, to destroy the enemy.

DAVID'S MOMENTUM

> I have pursued mine enemies, and overtaken them: neither did I turn again till they were consumed....Then did I beat them small as the dust before the wind: I did cast them out as the dirt in the streets.
>
> —PSALM 18:37–42, KJV

David knew how to get momentum and use it against the enemy. Once he got the upper hand, he pressed the battle and did not turn until he consumed his enemies. He did not stop with a slight victory; he rode his momentum until he slaughtered the enemy. David understood the importance of momentum.

Once the Lord gives you momentum, you must use it to your advantage. Don't stop after a slight victory. Continue until the enemy is routed, and you have won.

Once David had his enemies on the run, he pursued and overtook them. He consumed them and beat them "as the dust before the wind." He allowed nothing to stop his momentum. He knew his momentum came from the Lord. He knew that once the Lord gave it to him, he had to use it to fulfill His purpose.

There are too many of the Lord's people who stop after a victory. Instead of using that victory as momentum for the next battle, they relax and lose it. The period following a victory is not the time to relax. There are more battles to fight and victories to be won. There are Goliaths to face after you defeat your lion and your bear.

Be like David. Pursue, overtake, and consume the enemy! Be persistent and press the battle. Once the Lord gives you the upper hand, have no mercy on Satan and his demons. Use your momentum to your advantage.

Momentum Gives You Strength to Succeed in Long Seasons of Battle

> Now there was long war between the house of Saul and the house of David: but David waxed stronger and stronger, and the house of Saul waxed weaker and weaker.
>
> —2 Samuel 3:1, kjv

> And David went on and became great, and the Lord God of hosts was with him.
>
> —2 Samuel 5:10

Those who get momentum will prevail. David eventually gained momentum in his war with the house of Saul. The Rotherham Translation says he "went on and on waxing great." The American translation says, "Kept on increasing in power."

In the long struggle between David and Saul, it looked at times as if David would lose his life. David even said himself, "I shall perish someday by the hand of Saul" (1 Sam. 27:1). David found himself fleeing Saul and dwelling in the land of the Philistines, the enemy's camp.

Saul pursued David in the caves and mountains of Israel, and the Lord graciously delivered David from his enemy. After the death of Saul there was a long war between David and Saul's son, Ishbosheth. Abner, the captain of Ishbosheth's army, fought against Joab, the captain of David's army.

Now David begins to get momentum. He gets stronger and stronger, while his enemies get weaker and weaker.

The Scripture states that David went on and grew "great." His momentum not only carried him to the throne to be king over Israel, but it also carried him to victory over Israel's enemies.

> And David did so, as the Lord had commanded him; and smote the Philistines from Geba until thou come to Gazer.
>
> —2 Samuel 5:25, kjv

> And after this it came to pass that David smote the Philistines, and subdued them: and David took Methegammah out of the hand of the Philistines.
>
> And he smote Moab, and measured them with a line, casting them down to the ground....
>
> David smote also Hadadezer, the son of Rehob, king of Zobah....
>
> David slew of the Syrians two and twenty thousand men....
>
> And all they of Edom became David's servants.
>
> —2 Samuel 8:1–3, 5, 14, kjv

David was, what we call today *on a roll*. He harnessed his momentum and maintained it to defeat his enemies within Israel and without. Each victory gave him increased momentum for his next challenge.

We go from strength to strength, faith to faith, and glory to glory.

The Dark Side to Momentum

Not only can momentum work for you, but it can also work against you. Even wickedness, if not stopped, will gain momentum. David's momentum of victories came to an end because of his sin of adultery with Bathsheba and the murder of Uriah, her husband. This opened the door for the enemy to use his son, Absalom, against him. Absalom gained momentum against his father. His conspiracy grew stronger and stronger.

> And the conspiracy grew strong, for the people with Absalom continually increased in number.
>
> —2 Samuel 15:12

This shows us the power of momentum. Once anything gains momentum, whether good or evil, it is hard to stop. Because David was not able to nip it in the bud, the conspiracy of Absalom grew stronger and gained momentum.

> And there came a messenger to David, saying, The hearts of the men of Israel are after Absalom. And David said unto all his servants that were with him at Jerusalem, Arise, and let us flee; for we shall not else escape from Absalom: make speed to depart, lest he overtake us suddenly.
>
> —2 SAMUEL 15:13–14, KJV

David had to flee for his life. The momentum for evil was so strong that he did not have the strength to stop it. Only David's prayers and God's intervention were strong enough to stop Absalom's momentum.

David gave his enemies momentum against him through his foolishness. Sin can not only stop your momentum, but it can also give the enemy momentum against you. This is why it is imperative that we maintain our momentum by avoiding sin and foolishness. Give no place to the devil (Eph. 4:27).

Keep your momentum over the enemy. Never allow him to get momentum over you. One sinful act can destroy your momentum. One foolish act can destroy your momentum. One costly mistake can stop your momentum.

One Achan stopped Israel's momentum. One sin stopped David's momentum.

> And it came to pass, after the year was expired, at the time when kings go forth to battle, that David sent Joab....But David tarried still at Jerusalem.
>
> —2 SAMUEL 11:1, KJV

This was the beginning of David's troubles. Instead of going forth to battle as the leader of God's people, he stayed at Jerusalem and sent Joab to battle. David had just slain the Syrians, destroying seven hundred chariots and forty thousand horsemen to a previous battle (2 Sam. 10:18). This gives us an important truth: Don't stop after a victory. Keep your momentum! Remember, a victory gives you momentum for the next battle.

Instead of going forth into battle, David remained in Jerusalem and fell into adultery with Bathsheba (2 Sam. 11:2–5). David relaxed and fell into sin. He lost his momentum, and his string of victories came to an end. This opened the way for the enemy to bring much sadness and grief into his life. David almost lost his kingdom as a result. This hidden sin stopped his momentum. Although he tried to hide it and cover it up, it caused him eventual shame and dishonor.

THE LORD OF BURSTS

> And David came to Baalperazim, and David smote them there, and said, The LORD hath broken forth upon mine enemies before me, as a breach of waters…
>
> —2 SAMUEL 5:20, KJV

David describes his momentum from the Lord as a "breach of waters." The Rotherham translation says, "like a breaking forth of waters." The Moffat translation says, "like waters bursting a dam." He called the name of the place "Baalperazim," which means *lord of bursts*.

To burst means to force open (as a door) by strong or vigorous action. It means to break open, apart, or into pieces—usually from impact or from pressure within. Remember, the key to impact is momentum. The greater the momentum, the greater the impact. The Lord wants to give you so much momentum that you literally burst forth upon your enemies.

When a dam breaks, the momentum from the rushing waters will destroy everything in its path. Your momentum can be like a mighty rushing river, destroying and overtaking any opposition from the devil in your path.

THE POWER OF GOD THRUSTS YOU INTO MOMENTUM

> Behold, I send the Promise of My Father upon you; but tarry in the city of Jerusalem until you are endued with power from on high.
>
> —LUKE 24:49

The church started with momentum. The Day of Pentecost was a day of momentum for the church. *Dunamis* is the Greek word for power. Dunamis gives the church momentum.

Momentum is the result of power. The more powerful a thing becomes, the more momentum it carries, and the more momentum a thing receives the more power it has. Momentum and impact are related to thrust. *To thrust* means to push or drive with force. The force needed to thrust the church forward was *dunamis*, the power of the Holy Ghost.

The Day of Pentecost gave the church the momentum it needed to invade the world with the gospel. From Jerusalem the church moved forward with and maintained its momentum to impact the world with the message of salvation.

> That day about three thousand souls were added to them.
> —Acts 2:41

> Howbeit many of them which heard the word believed; and the number of the men was about five thousand.
> —Acts 4:4, kjv

> Believers were increasingly added to the Lord, multitudes of both men and women.
> —Acts 5:14

> There came also a multitude out of the cities round about unto Jerusalem, bringing sick folks, and them which were vexed with unclean spirits; and they were healed every one. Then the high priest rose up, and all they that were with him, (which is the sect of the Sadducees) and were filled with indignation.
> —Acts 5:16–17, kjv

Persecution is an attempt by the enemy to stop momentum. The first opposition the early church encountered was from the established religious system of their day. Every revival and move of God is fought by religion. Those who want to maintain the status quo don't like change. We   must   have   enough   momentum   to   break   through persecution. Never allow persecution for righteousness sake to stop your momentum. Never allow what people say or do stop your momentum, if you are in the will of God. Recognize persecution as an attempt by Satan to stop your momentum. You cannot react to it in the flesh; you must respond to it in the Spirit.

> And when they had called the apostles and beaten them, they commanded that they should not speak in the name of Jesus, and let them go. And they departed from the presence of the council, rejoicing that they were counted worthy to suffer shame for his name.
> —Acts 5:40–41, kjv

The apostles did not allow the persecution to stop their momentum. They responded to a physical beating by rejoicing. "Daily in the temple, and in every house, they did not cease teaching and preaching Jesus as the Christ" (Acts 5:42).

They did not cease to teach and preach. Once you gain momentum in any endeavor, don't cease! Learning how to maintain your momentum in the face of opposition is a key to your success.

THE RESULT OF MOMENTUM

Even after threats and beatings from the religious leader, the apostles kept their momentum.

> And the word of God increased; and the number of disciples multiplied in Jerusalem greatly; and a great company of the priests were obedient to the faith.
> —Acts 6:7, kjv

Increase and multiplication are the result of momentum. Even the strongest opponent of the church, Saul, was changed and became the apostle Paul. This shows us the power of momentum. The enemy will not be able to stop a person with momentum. When the Lord's people gain momentum, it will cause our enemies to either be destroyed or converted.

After the conversion of Saul, the church had rest throughout all Judea, Galilee, and Samaria, and "were multiplied" (Acts 9:31). When a move of God gains momentum, it will sweep everything in its path. People will either be swept into it or be destroyed by it.

In Acts 12:1–3 we see how Herod was used by the enemy to stop the church's momentum. We see here that another way the enemy stops the momentum of a move of God is to attack its leaders.

Every move of God has leaders. Herod killed James and was planning to kill Peter. The church prayed day and night for Peter's release. Because of angelic intervention, Peter was set free from prison. Not only did an angel deliver Peter, but an angel also smote Herod, and he was eaten by worms (Acts 12:23).

If the enemy can discourage or eliminate a leader, he is often successful in stopping the momentum of a move.

> But the word of God grew and multiplied.
> —ACTS 12:24

The Phillips translation says, "But the word of the Lord continued to gain ground and increase its influence." Herod was destroyed, and the church maintained its momentum. Leaders need prayer. They need intercessors to stand with them in order to keep their momentum. Intercession and prayer help us maintain momentum in the face of opposition.

BOLDNESS HELPS YOU MAINTAIN MOMENTUM

> And now, Lord, behold their threatenings: and grant unto thy servants, that with all boldness they may speak thy word. By stretching forth thine hand to heal; and that signs and wonders may be done by the name of thy holy child Jesus.
> —ACTS 4:29–30, KJV

The threatening of the religious leaders was intended to stop the momentum of the early church. They prayed for boldness that would result from signs and wonders. Fear will stop your momentum. The fear of man brings a snare. Fear will paralyze you. It is a spirit from hell, sent to stop you. Boldness must rise up in your spirit to overcome opposition. Anyone who gains momentum will encounter resistance.

The enemy will not just sit back and watch you go forth and establish the kingdom of God without resistance. He will attempt to stop you through fear. Boldness helps us maintain momentum. Instead of drawing back, the apostles "were all filled with the Holy Ghost, and they spake the word of God with boldness" (Acts 4:31, KJV).

Through boldness they overcame the opposition of the enemy. Many believers give up the moment they encounter resistance. They lose their momentum and stop doing what the Lord has commanded them to do. Pray for boldness. Rise up in courage and continue in spite of intimidation.

> And when they had gone through the isle unto Paphos, they found a certain sorcerer, a false prophet, a Jew, whose name was Barjesus.
>
> —ACTS 13:6, KJV

If the enemy cannot stop you through fear and intimidation, he will attempt to stop you through deception. Paul and Barnabas encountered a sorcerer named Barjesus on their first missionary journey. Barjesus, also known as Elymas, withstood them (Acts 13:8). Paul called judgment down upon Barjesus, who was smitten blind.

Paul called him, "O full of all deceit and all fraud" (Acts 13:10). The Twentieth Century New Testament says: "You incarnation of deceit and fraud!" The Williams translation says: "You expert in every form of deception and sleight-of-hand."

Satan will use men to stop your momentum. One bad relationship can stop your momentum. One good relationship can give you momentum.

When the Israelites came out of Egypt, they had momentum. When Balak (the king of Moab) saw the people of Israel, he called for Balaam to come and curse them. He tried to use witchcraft to stop their progress.

MIRACLES GIVE YOU MOMENTUM

Miracles have the power to release momentum. The Lord desires to work miracles through His people to give us the momentum we need to make an impact for God. Miracles have the power to sweep multitudes into the kingdom in a short period of time. The ministry of Jesus impacted the entire nation because of miracles.

> And Jesus went about all Galilee, teaching in their synagogues, preaching the gospel of the kingdom, and healing all kinds of sickness and all kinds of disease among the people.
>
> Then His fame went throughout all Syria; and they brought to Him all sick people who were afflicted with various diseases and torments, and those who were demon-possessed, epileptics, and paralytics; and He healed them.
>
> Great multitudes followed Him—from Galilee, and from Decapolis, Jerusalem, Judea, and beyond the Jordan.
> —MATTHEW 4:23–25

The ministry of Jesus gained tremendous momentum because of the miracles He performed. It was not long before multitudes of people followed Him. Jesus gained such momentum that the religious leaders figured only His death would stop it. They plotted to kill Jesus in order to stop His momentum.

> Then gathered the chief priests and the Pharisees a council, and said, What do we? for this man doeth many miracles. If we let him thus alone, all men will believe on him: and the Romans shall come and take away both our place and nation.
> —JOHN 11:47–48, KJV

> Much people of the Jews therefore knew that he was there: and they came not for Jesus' sake only, but that they might

> see Lazarus also, whom he had raised from the dead. But the chief priests consulted that they might put Lazarus also to death; because that by reason of him many of the Jews went away, and believed on Jesus. On the next day much people that were come to the feast, when they heard that Jesus was coming to Jerusalem, took branches of palm trees, and went forth to meet him, and cried, Hosanna: Blessed is the King of Israel that cometh in the name of the Lord.... The Pharisees therefore said among themselves, perceive ye how ye prevail nothing? behold, the word is gone after him.

> —John 12:9–13, 19, kjv

The raising of Lazarus from the dead was the straw that broke the camel's back. The religious leaders were so upset and worried about the momentum of Jesus's ministry that they even consulted to put Lazarus to death. There is no substitute for miracles.

Miracles are a manifestation of God's power in the earth that breaks the power of demonic strongholds and sets people free to receive the truth of the gospel. People will always be attracted to miracles. There is something in all of us that desires to see the supernatural. Some have called healing and miracles God's dinner bell to salvation.

When the religious leaders were attempting to stop the momentum of the early church, the prayer of God's people was for the Lord to stretch forth His hand to heal and perform signs and wonders in the name of Jesus (Acts 4:30).

Signs and wonders not only give us momentum, but they also help us maintain momentum. A church with miracles is a church that will continue to march triumphantly throughout the land.

One deliverance. One miracle. One healing. One vision. One prophetic word. One relationship is all it takes to start momentum. One sermon you hear. One conference you attend. One prophetic word you receive...can break you through and give you the momentum you need to go forth and be victorious.

Don't despise the day of small things. Hurricanes start out as small storms that pick up momentum. You may not be doing much now, but take a step at a time and pick up momentum as you go. Once you receive and maintain momentum it will carry you great distances.

PRAYERS THAT RELEASE THE POWER OF THE LORD

Lord, release Your glorious power against the enemy (Exod. 15:6).

Let power and might be released from Your hand (1 Chron. 29:12).

Scatter the enemy by Your power (Ps. 59:11).

Rule over Your enemies through Your power (Ps. 66:7).

Let the power of Your anger be released against the powers of darkness (Ps. 90:11).

I release the power and authority of the Lord against all demons I encounter in the name of Jesus (Matt. 10:1).

I am delivered from the power of Satan unto God (Acts 26:18).

Divide the sea, and destroy marine spirits through Your power (Job 26:12).

I am strong in the Lord and in the power of His might (Eph. 6:10).

Cause the powers of darkness to submit to Your power.

Display Your awesome power that men will believe.

Release Your power in healing and deliverance (Luke 5:17).

Release Your powerful voice (Ps. 29:4).

Let me be amazed at Your power (Luke 9:43).

Let great power be released through Your apostles (Acts 4:33).

Let signs, wonders, and miracles be released through the power of the Holy Spirit (Rom. 15:19).

Let me preach and teach with demonstration of the Spirit and power (1 Cor. 2:4).

Let Your power work in me (Eph. 3:20).

Release Your powerful angels on my behalf to fight my battles in the heavens (2 Pet. 2:11; Rev. 18:1).

Release the power of Elijah through Your prophets (Luke 1:17).

Let me be willing in the day of Your power (Ps. 110:3).

PRAYERS FOR BOLDNESS AND COURAGE

I am bold as a lion (Prov. 28:1).

I have boldness and access with confidence by faith in Christ (Eph. 3:12).

I have much boldness in Christ (Philem. 1:8).

I have boldness to enter the holy place by the blood of Jesus (Heb. 10:19).

Lord, grant me the boldness that I may speak forth (Acts. 4:29).

Lord, I pray with all prayers and supplication that I may open my mouth boldly to make known the mysteries of the gospel (Eph. 6:19).

Let me be much more bold to speak the Word without fear (Phil. 1:14).

I have great boldness in the faith of Christ Jesus (1 Tim. 3:13).

I come boldly to the throne of grace, that I may obtain mercy, and find grace to help in time of need (Heb. 4:16).

I boldly say, "The Lord is my helper, and I will not fear what man will do to me" (Heb. 13:6).

I have boldness in the day of judgment: because as he is, so am I in this world (1 John 4:17).

Let men see my boldness and know that I have been with Jesus (Acts. 4:13).

Let me be filled with the Holy Ghost that I may speak the word of God with boldness (Acts 4:31).

I will wait on the Lord and be of good courage and He will strengthen my heart (Ps. 27:14).

I will be strong and courageous; I will not be afraid, for the Lord is with me wherever I go (Josh. 1:9).

I will be courageous to keep and do all that the Lord has told me (Josh. 23:6).

I take courage.

I will deal courageously and the Lord will be with me (2 Chron. 19:11).

CHAPTER 6
THIEVES THAT COME TO KILL AND DESTROY A GOOD LIFE

The thief does not come, except to steal and kill and destroy.

—JOHN 10:10, MEV

ADOLF HITLER AND Nazi Germany had momentum at the beginning for World War II. Through a battle plan called "blitzkrieg," they were able to invade countries through the element of surprise and win quick, easy victories. Germany was winning the war through momentum. However, the Allies eventually stopped Hitler's momentum.

A turning point in World War II was the battle of Stalingrad in Russia. Temperatures plunged to forty degrees below zero. Troops lacked warm clothing and suffered frostbite. Tanks and weapons broke down. The Russian winter stopped Hitler's troops and over three hundred thousand were killed or captured. From that point, the momentum began to change, and it was only a matter of time before Hitler and Germany fell.

Hitler could have learned from Napoleon that a Russian winter can stop an army's momentum. Napoleon's armies swept across Europe in the early 1800s. Because of his momentum his armies were unstoppable. But his momentum was stopped by a Russian winter when he decided to invade Moscow. Of the six hundred thousand men in Napoleon's forces, over five hundred thousand were killed, captured, or died from illness.

There are Russian winters in the spirit that can stop our momentum and get us off focus from realizing victory and success in various areas of our lives. I mentioned in the previous chapter that a lack of wisdom is a sure way to see trouble come into your life and miss out on life's opportunities. Getting wisdom is your responsibility. You can ask God for it, and He will give it to you freely. Then there is the work of the enemy.

The Bible says that the devil does not come but to steal, kill, and destroy (John 10:10). He has set a strategy against you to keep you from being all that God created you to be. It is important to know what traps the devil has set to steal your peace. Knowing what those traps are will give you the edge you need to resist him and maintain your position of victory. (See Ephesians 6:11; James 4:7; 2 Corinthians 2:11.)

CONTROLLERS AND MANIPULATORS

> O foolish Galatians! Who has bewitched you that you should not obey the truth…
> —GALATIANS 3:1

> Ye did run well; who did hinder you that ye should not obey the truth?
> —GALATIANS 5:7, KJV

The Knox translation says: "Senseless Galatians, who is it that has cast a spell on you…?"

Coming under the control of another is witchcraft, which puts you under a spell. The Goodspeed translation of Galatians 5:7 says: "You were making such progress!"

Beware of wrong relationships. Controllers and manipulators will stop your momentum. The Galatians had lost their momentum by allowing themselves to come under the control of legalistic teachers. Beware of legalism. It will stop your spiritual momentum.

Stand fast in liberty. Maintain your liberty and freedom in the Spirit. Stay free in the Spirit. Follow the cloud of God. Some people are stuck in previous moves of God. They stopped to build a monument. They refused to move on with God into the next move. Every move of God is designed to give you momentum for the next move. Let nothing stop you from obeying God.

Religious control will stop your momentum. Too many believers allow religious control to stop them. Control spirits are from the devil. Relationships based on fear, control, and intimidation are of the devil. Relationships from God will help you get and maintain your momentum. Relationships from the devil will cause you to stop and lose your momentum.

HIDDEN SIN

> So about three thousand men went up there from the people, but they fled before the men of Ai. And the men of Ai struck down about thirty-six men, for they chased them from before the gate as far as Shebarim, and struck them down on the descent; therefore the hearts of the people melted and became like water.
>
> —JOSHUA 7:4–5

Ai was the second battle Israel fought after they entered Canaan. The first battle was Jericho. They destroyed Jericho and seemed to have the momentum they needed to defeat Ai. Even though Ai seemed to be an easy victory in the natural, they were turned back in defeat. Achan had brought a curse upon Israel by partaking of the accursed thing.

As a result, Israel could not stand before their enemies. Because of one man's trespass Israel lost their momentum. They were brought to a virtual standstill. Joshua had to pray to receive revelation as to why Israel fell before Ai.

Joshua 7:1 calls this the act of "trespass." The word *trespass* is the Hebrew word *maal* meaning sin, falsehood, transgression. It also means treachery, to act covertly or treacherously, to cover up. This is exactly what Achan did. He tried to cover up his sin by hiding the garment of silver he had coveted.

This gives us a clue as to what stops us short of achieving good success. Not only does sin stop us, but *hidden* sins can do the most damage. The hidden sin of Achan stopped the momentum and forward progress of Joshua and the armies of Israel.

Jericho was a great victory. After Jericho fell, every nation in Canaan heard of its defeat. This great victory gave Israel the momentum it needed to go forth and possess Canaan. Remember, every victory gives you momentum for the next battle. Israel should have had no problem with Ai. It was a small city compared to Jericho. The Israelites were so sure of victory that they did not send their entire army against it. But the defeat by Ai came as a result of a hidden sin.

Hidden sins will destroy your movement toward victory. Anything that can hinder your success in God needs to be eliminated from your life. Any relationship, habit, or act that leads you into sin, must be eliminated from your life if you are to maintain your spiritual momentum.

Ask yourself this: What is the one thing that always keeps me from moving forward? Is it a particular habit that I cannot seem to break? Is it a relationship that I cannot seem to shake? Is it anger, lust, fear, discouragement, depression, hurt, bitterness, unforgiveness?

Whatever it is that stops your momentum, you must isolate it and eliminate it from your life. There is no hidden sin worth keeping you from the things God's covenant provides.

PROCRASTINATION

Jesus knew at an early age that He must be about His Father's business. Some people always dream about tomorrow without ever doing anything today. What you do today will determine whether you will have success tomorrow. Success comes as a result of action.

Procrastinators are full of excuses. You must eliminate every excuse that stops you from doing what you have been called to do. Moses's excuse was his speech. Jeremiah's was his youth. There is no excuse worth stopping your movement toward success in God. God's grace is sufficient. Winners don't allow excuses to stop them from winning.

PASSIVITY AND SLOTHFULNESS

> Slothfulness gradually prevails over the faithful unless it be corrected.[1]
>
> —Jean Calvin

Some people are too passive and lazy to maintain a successful and victorious life. Successful people are doers of the Word (James 1:22). Slothfulness is apathy, dullness, idleness, indolence, languor, laziness, lethargy, lifelessness, listlessness, passivity, slowness, sluggishness, tiredness. Slothfulness is an aversion to work or exertion. A slothful person has the characteristics of a sloth. A sloth is slow-moving and stationary animal.

Slothfulness will put you in bondage. "The hand of the diligent shall bear rule: but the slothful shall be under tribute" (Prov. 12:24, kjv).

The sluggard is entangled. The way of the sluggard is painful. "The way of the sluggard is overgrown with thorns [it pricks, lacerates, and entangles him], but the way of the righteous is plain and raised like a highway" (Prov. 15:19, amp).

Slothfulness opens the door for poverty. "Slothfulness casteth into a deep sleep; and an idle soul shall suffer hunger" (Prov. 19:15, kjv).

Slothfulness can open you up to death. "The desire of the lazy man kills him, for his hands refuse to labor" (Prov. 21:25).

Slothfulness will cause your life to fall apart. Slothfulness leads to decay. "I went by the field of the slothful, and by the vineyard of the man void of understanding; and, lo, it was all grown over with thorns, and nettles had covered the face thereof, and the stone wall thereof was broken down" (Prov. 24:30–31, kjv). Then Ecclesiastes 10:18 says, "Because of laziness the building decays, and through idleness of hands the house leaks."

If we want to experience the full provision of the covenant operating in our lives, then we cannot be slothful and passive. There are pieces to the puzzle that require work. We must not be slow to act when God is telling us to move. We are commanded in Romans 12:11 not to be slothful in business but to be "fervent in spirit, serving the Lord."

Winning the battle of the bed

The bed can become your worst enemy. There are many people trapped by the bed. Sleep can be your worst enemy. Everyone needs sleep, but many sleep too much, and many are spiritually asleep. You must win the battle of the bed if you want to succeed in life. You must be able to rise and pray when necessary.

> Laziness casts one into a deep sleep, and an idle person will suffer hunger.
>
> —Proverbs 19:15

The Bible talks about the dangers of slothfulness. In Matthew 26:40 it tells of the time when Jesus asked His disciples to pray with Him, but when He came back to check on them, He found them asleep. He asked them, "What! Could you not watch with Me one hour?" The disciples were sleeping when they should have been praying. The battle of the bed will translate into a lack of prayer.

Excessive sleep, like slothfullness, will open the door to poverty. Proverbs 6:9–11 says:

> How long will you slumber, O sluggard? When will you rise from your sleep? A little sleep, a little slumber, a little folding of the hands to sleep—so shall your poverty come on you like a prowler, and your need like an armed man.

Proverbs 20:13 says, "Do not love sleep, lest you come to poverty; open your eyes, and you will be satisfied with bread."

Deep sleep can be the judgment of God: "For the Lord has poured out on you the spirit of deep sleep, and has closed your eyes, namely, the prophets; and He has covered your heads, namely, the seers" (Isa. 29:10).

Watchmen should not be asleep: "His watchmen are blind: they are all ignorant, they are all dumb dogs, they cannot bark; sleeping, lying down, loving to slumber" (Isa. 56:10).

Sleep can open you up to temptation. When Jesus rose from His prayer and returned to His disciples, He found them sleeping and said to them, "Why do you sleep? Rise and pray, lest you enter into temptation" (Luke 22:46). First Thessalonians 5:6 says, "Therefore let us not sleep, as others do, but let us watch and be sober."

There is a spirit of slumber: "As it is written: 'God has given them a spirit of stupor, eyes that they should not see and ears that they should not hear, to this very day'" (Rom. 11:8).

Many look to the bed for comfort: "When I say, My bed shall comfort me, my couch shall ease my complaints" (Job 7:13, KJV).

Some use the bed to meditate in the night watches: "When I remember thee upon my bed, and meditate on thee in the night watches" (Psalm 63:6, KJV).

David won the battle of the bed. Could this be the secret to so many of his victories? Psalm 132:1–5 reads, "LORD, remember David, and all his afflictions; how he swore to the LORD, and vowed to the Mighty One of Jacob: 'Surely I will not go into the chamber of my house, or go up to the comfort of my bed; I will not give sleep to my eyes or slumber to my eyelids, until I find a place for the LORD, a dwelling place for the Mighty One of Jacob.'"

Seasons of prayer through the night watches allow us to reflect on God's working in our lives and gives us time to meditate on His Word: "At midnight I will rise to give thanks to You, because of Your righteous judgments" (Ps. 119:62). And Psalm 119:148 says, "My eyes are awake through the night watches, that I may meditate on Your word."

There are sleep disorders that keep people tied to the bed, and there is fear that paralyzes and keeps one asleep and inactive. Laziness is another factor that has no place in a believer's life. Pray and ask God for wisdom on how to be delivered from slothfulness and a spirit of slumber. Fasting and prayer is a good spiritual strategy to gain victory over the bed. See chapter 7 for more on fasting.

DOUBLE-MINDEDNESS

A double-minded man is unstable in all of his ways.

—JAMES 1:8, MEV

Some people never reach a place of success because they never decide to do anything. They are too indecisive. They can never make up their minds as to which direction they should go. The Goodspeed translation of James 1:8 describes the double-minded as "an irresolute person like him, who is uncertain about everything he does." The Weymouth translations says this is "being a man of two minds, undecided in every step he takes."

A good, favor-filled life does not come knocking at your door. You must take steps toward it. Receiving what God has promised to you always begins with a first step, a decision. Don't allow double-mindedness to keep you from taking the first step. Decide to do something. Be a person of action. Jesus knew his Father's will and moved in that direction. You may start off slow, but as you gain momentum, you will begin to see results. A thousand-mile journey begins with one small step.

HOW TO REGAIN YOUR MOMENTUM

> But mine enemies are lively, and they are strong: and they that hate me wrongfully are multiplied.
>
> —PSALM 38:19, KJV

When David sinned, he lost his momentum and gave his enemies an advantage. David's enemies had momentum against him. Either you have momentum or your enemy has momentum. David's sin caused him to lose his momentum. Absalom gained momentum and used it to attempt to take the kingdom. Throughout the Psalms David prayed and repented. This gives us an important key to regaining our momentum—repentance.

> O spare me, that I may recover strength, before I go hence, and be no more.
>
> —PSALM 39:13, KJV

When we have lost our momentum, and the enemy has gained momentum, we need the mercy of the Lord. Only the Lord can stop the enemy's momentum.

> Let them be driven backward and put to shame that
> wish me evil.
>   —Psalm 40:14, kjv

Prayer and fasting will help you regain your momentum. Prayer and fasting will lift up a standard against the enemy. Fasting turns back the armies of the enemy (Joel 2:20)

> I humbled my soul with fasting.
>   —Psalm 35:13, mev

> My knees are weak through fasting; and my flesh faileth
> of fatness.
>   —Psalm 109:24, kjv

When David's enemies prevailed, he used that key of fasting to stop the enemies' momentum. Through prayer and fasting he regained the ground he lost on his way to victory. The battle was turned against his enemies in his favor. Prayer and fasting causes the enemy to be turned back. You must have the knowledge to take away the enemy's momentum and regain yours. Even so, it is better to maintain your forward movement and never lose it.

On the other hand, if you have lost your momentum, don't give up! There is a way to regain it through repentance, prayer, and fasting. We must remember that our God is the Father of mercies (2 Cor. 1:3). We can come boldly to the throne of grace and obtain mercy, and find grace to help in the time of need (Heb. 4:16).

The Lord will hear your prayer, release His mercy, restore you, and cause you to regain your momentum. If you have lost your momentum, spend some time in fasting and prayer, which I will talk about more in the next chapter. Through fasting you will begin to see your spiritual and physical life invigorated.

Although David fell, he knew the Lord was merciful. David's repentance, prayer, and fasting caused him to regain his place on the road to lasting victory to live the life that he had been anointed for and to be restored in God's kingdom.

Never Again Confessions That Block Thieves of Success and Prosperity

Never again will I allow poverty and lack to control my life, for my God supplies all my need according to His riches in glory by Christ Jesus (Phil. 4:19).

Never again will I lack, for I have plenty (Gen. 27:28).

Never again will I lack, for I will have plenty of silver (Job 22:25).

Never again will I lack; I will be plenteous in goods (Deut. 28:11).

Never again will I lack, but I will prosper through prophetic ministry (Ezra 6:14).

Never again will I sow and not reap, but I will reap where others have sown (John 4:38).

Never again will I carry a bag full of holes (Hag. 1:6).

Never will I lack glory (*kabowd*), honor, abundance, riches, splendor, glory, dignity, reputation, and reverence (Ps. 84:11).

Never again will I be poor, for the Lord became poor that I through His poverty might be rich (2 Cor. 8:9).

Never again will I live without the desires of my heart, because I will delight myself in the Lord (Ps. 37:4).

Never again will I allow covetousness to control my life, but I am a liberal giver (Prov. 11:25).

Never again will the enemy devour my finances, for the Lord has rebuked the devourer for my sake (Mal. 3:11).

Never again will I hold back from giving, for I give, and it is given to me, good measure, pressed down, shaken together, and running over do men give to me (Luke 6:38).

Never again will I allow fear to stop me from giving.

Never again will I allow debt to control my life, for I will lend unto many nations and not borrow, for the borrower is servant to the lender (Prov. 22:7).

Never again will I allow doubt and unbelief to stop me from believing in the promises of God (Heb. 3:19).

Never again will I think poverty and lack, for as a man thinks in his heart, so is he (Prov. 23:7).

Never again will my basket and store be empty, for my basket and store are blessed (Deut. 28:5, KJV).

Never again will I allow slothfulness and laziness to dominate my life, for slothfulness casts into a deep sleep (Prov. 19:15, KJV).

Never again will I allow Satan to steal my finances, but I have abundant life (John 10:10).

Never again will I limit what God can do in my finances and in my life (Ps. 78:41).

Never again will I tolerate lack, for my God gives me abundance (Deut. 28:47).

Never again will I have just enough, for El Shaddai gives me more than enough (Gen. 17:1–2).

Never again will I use my money for sinful things (Ezek. 16:17).

Never again will the enemy hold back my blessings.

Never again will I doubt God's desire to prosper me, for the Lord takes pleasure in the prosperity of His servant (Ps. 35:27).

Never again will I be the tail and not the head (Deut. 28:13).

Never again will I be a borrower and not a lender (Deut. 28:12).

Never again will I be behind and not in front (Deut. 25:18).

Never again will I believe I don't have power to get wealth, for God gives me power to get wealth to establish His covenant (Deut. 8:18).

Never again will I lack any good thing, because I will seek the Lord (Ps. 34:10).

Never again will I lack prosperity, but whatever I do will prosper, because I delight in the law of the Lord (Ps. 1).

Never again will I lack anointing for my head (Eccles. 9:8).

Never again will I allow the circumstances to steal my joy, for the joy of the Lord is my strength (Neh. 8:10).

Never again will I lack favor for my life, for with favor the Lord will surround me as a shield (Ps. 5:12).

Never again will I walk in the flesh instead of walking in the Spirit (Gal. 5:16).

Never again will I allow my flesh to do what it wants. I am crucified with Christ (Gal. 2:20).

Never again will I walk in the works of the flesh, but I will manifest the fruit of the Spirit (Gal. 5:22–23).

Never again will I be weak, for I am strong (Joel 3:10).

Never again will I be oppressed, for I am far from oppression (Isa. 54:14).

Never again will I be depressed.

Never again will I vexed and tormented by demons, for I have been delivered from the power of darkness and translated in the kingdom of God's dear Son (Col. 1:13, KJV).

Never again will I allow perversion and sexual immorality to control my life; I flee fornication (1 Cor. 6:18).

Never again will I enjoy that which is forbidden by the Lord (2 Cor. 6:17).

Never again will I allow worldliness and carnality to control my life (1 John 2:15).

Never again will I conform to the world (Rom. 12:2).

Never again will I allow anger to control my life, but I am slow to anger and sin not (Prov. 16:32; James 1:19).

Never again will I get angry at another person's success, but I rejoice in the success of others (Rom. 12:10, 15).

Never again will I allow unforgiveness and bitterness to control my life (Eph. 4:31).

Never again will I allow discouragement and depression to dominate my life, but I will praise Him who is the health of my countenance (Ps. 42:5).

Never again will I allow jealousy and envy to enter my heart, for envy is the rottenness of the bones (Prov. 14:30).

CHAPTER 7

BREAKTHROUGH TO LIFE AND FAVOR THROUGH FASTING AND PRAYER

*Now on the twenty-fourth day of this month the children of Israel
were assembled with fasting, in sackcloth, and with dust on their
heads. . . . "And because of all this, we make a sure covenant and
write it; our leaders, our Levites, and our priests seal it."*

—NEHEMIAH 9:1, 38

FASTING IS A way we can renew covenant with the Lord and experience His favor on our lives. Fasting helps fallen believers become restored. Fasting is a part of renewing our commitment to the things of God. Fasting has great rewards. Many believers are unaware of the great rewards that come through fasting. Understanding the great benefits of fasting will motivate more believers to make it a regular part of their lives.

Fasting is also one of the ways to increase the breaker anointing. Do you have things in your life or in the lives of your family members that need to be broken? Fasting can release the breaker anointing. The prophet Micah prophesied the day of the breaker coming up before his people. We are living in the days of the breaker.

> The breaker is come up before them: they have broken up,
> and have passed through the gate, and are gone out by it:
> and their king shall pass before them, and the LORD on
> the head of them.
>
> —MICAH 2:13, KJV

The Lord is a breaker. He is able to break through any obstacle or opposition on behalf of His covenant people. There is a breaker anointing arising in the church. We are seeing and experiencing more breakthroughs than ever before. Fasting will cause breakthroughs to continue in families, cities, nations, finances, church growth, salvation, healing, and deliverance. It will help believers to break through all opposition from the enemy.

There are some spirits operating in our lives that cannot be overcome without fasting. Some believers struggle with certain limitations that they cannot seem to break through. A revelation for how covenant and fasting work hand in hand will change this and result in victories and success that would not ordinarily be obtained. A life of consistent fasting will cause many victories to manifest. God's will is that His covenant believers live a life of victory and perfect peace with nothing being impossible to them.

As we learn from Matthew 17:21, there are stubborn spirits that will only respond to fasting and prayer. These tend to be the generational strongholds that tenaciously hold on to families and nations for years. These strongholds include poverty, sickness, witchcraft, sexual impurity, pride, fear, confusion, and marital problems. Fasting will help you overcome these strongholds and break free from their limitations.

> "Now, therefore," says the LORD, "Turn to Me with all your heart, with fasting, with weeping, and with mourning." So rend your heart, and not your garments; return to the LORD your God, for He is gracious and merciful, slow to anger, and of great kindness; and He relents from doing harm.
>
> —JOEL 2:12–13

Demons that come against your life are different in terms of their wickedness. There are demons that are more wicked, more unclean, stronger, more stubborn, and higher in rank, ability, and intelligence. The longer a demon has been in a family or in a person's life, the harder it is to remove because its roots go very deep. Demons such as rebellion, pride, witchcraft, Jezebel, poverty, and lack may only come out with a high level of faith.

Sometimes it seems as if these demons cannot be dislodged, and people will get discouraged and frustrated and feel they have failed. In Matthew 17 the disciples of Jesus encountered a demon in a young boy and could not cure him because of their unbelief. Unbelief hinders us from dealing with strongholds. It takes faith to dislodge the enemy. Fasting helps you overcome unbelief and build strong faith.

This is the supernatural combination that Jesus gave His disciples in Matthew 17: prayer and fasting. I am not saying that when you fast you will earn brownie points with God or that you are working your way to enjoying God's blessings. We don't fast to be saved, to please God, or to go to heaven. There is no law that says if you don't fast you will go to hell. We fast for breakthrough and revival, for our success and victory in God, and for our family and loved ones. The weapons of our warfare are not carnal but mighty through God!

Some things take fasting *and* prayer. There is no other way around. There are kinds of demons that just don't give up. They are strong, proud, arrogant, and defiant. Sometimes you have to do something unusual, extraordinary, and beyond the norm to see breakthrough. Normal church, normal Christianity, normal preaching, and normal praying are not going to get the job done. Some little sweet prayer is not going to do. Religion won't get it done. It is going to take an anointing that destroys the yoke.

When you fast, the anointing increases in your life because you are enveloped in the Spirit. The authority of God, power of God, and faith of God come alive when you lay aside some things and fast. You will find yourself getting stronger and stronger. Shouting doesn't do it. It is the anointing that does it.

In Isaiah 58 we learn how we can fast to break every yoke to undo the heavy burdens. As we mentioned in chapter 6, there are some things that try to come against the plans of God for your life. They try to bind you and stop you. But fasting makes room so that the oppressed go free. Fasting breaks bondages and causes revival. When you are dealing with a serious issue—maybe you are dealing with something you don't know how to handle—the best thing to do sometimes is to let go of some food for a little while. Pray against that thing. Man may not be able to help you and you may not know how to defeat it, but with God all things are possible.

As you fast and humble yourself, the grace of God will come upon your life. The Lord will be the strength of your life. What you could not do in the flesh you can do by the Spirit of God. Because it's not by might nor by power, but by the Spirit of the Lord that every mountain is removed!

Listen, extraordinary situations require extraordinary measures. Sometimes it only happens when you get desperate—when you are so tired of being defeated and hindered in an area.

Let's see some victories we haven't seen before. Let's get some breakthroughs we haven't had before. Let's see some miracles we haven't seen before. Let's drive out some demons we haven't driven out before. Let's see some curses broken that would not leave. Let's see some generational stuff uprooted that could not be uprooted. Let's see a change! Let's see our lives go in a positive direction. Let's see a life of abundance and not lack. Let's see peace and not strife.

You may have to fast, and not just once. Not twice. Not even three times. If you have to go more than that, go more than that. Don't give up. Keep doing it. Keep going until you know you have victory, until you have breakthrough, until you sense something breaking!

You have to get so tired of the devil that you say, "Enough is enough. If I have to turn my plate down to get a breakthrough in this area, I won't eat." When your stomach starts screaming out, tell it to back up. In the end you will win, and you will have victory! Let our spiritual enemies be smitten and consumed in Jesus's name!

You have to be determined: "No demon is going to control my life. I am a child of God and who the Son sets free is free indeed. I don't care how stubborn this thing is, how it tries to hang on. I am going to break every finger and the thumbs of the enemy. I'm going to break his wrists, break his grip.... Devil, you cannot have my life! I will see God's favor come upon my life!"

This is the faith and unshakable resolve fasting will build in your life to see deliverance in every area the enemy has tried to control.

Approach Fasting With Humility and Sincerity

In Jesus's day the Pharisees fasted with attitudes of pride and superiority:

> The Pharisee stood and prayed thus with himself, God, I thank thee, that I am not as other men are....I fast twice in the week...
>
> —Luke 18:11–12, kjv

Anytime you are full of pride, being legalistic and religious, you can fast and pray all you want, but you won't see many miracles. The Pharisees didn't have any miracles come as a result of their prayer and fasting. They had no power. Jesus had all the miracles because He was humble and full of mercy, love, and compassion toward people.

The Pharisees had nothing but long robes on. Robes with no miracles. They couldn't heal a headache. They couldn't heal a mosquito bite. They couldn't heal a hangnail. They had no power because they were not humble and showed no mercy. Jesus showed up and broke all their rules. He healed the sick, raised the dead, and cast out devils. Then they wanted to kill Him. They were not concerned about people. They were more concerned about their position and their title. Don't ever get to a place where your position or title takes the humility and the mercy of God out of your life. Always be humble. Always be merciful.

We must approach fasting with humility. Fasting must be genuine and not religious or hypocritical. This is what God requires in fasting. We must have correct motives in fasting. Fasting is a powerful tool if done correctly. Muslims and Hindus fast, but their fasts are merely religious. Great miracles and breakthroughs happen when fasting is done in the right spirit.

Isaiah chapter 58 describes the fast that God has chosen:

+ Fasting cannot be done with amusement (v. 3).
+ Fasting cannot be done while mistreating others (v. 3).
+ Fasting cannot be done for strife or contention (v. 4).
+ Fasting should cause one to bow his head in humility, like a bulrush (v. 5).
+ Fasting should be a time of searching the heart and repenting.
+ Fasting should be done with an attitude of compassion for the lost and hurting (v. 7).

This is the fast that God promises to bless.

The enemy knows the power of prayer and fasting, and he will do everything in his power to stop you. Believers who begin to fast can expect to encounter much spiritual resistance. A believer must be committed to a fasted lifestyle. The rewards of fasting far outweigh the obstacles of the enemy.

How to Fast

Fasting is beneficial whether you fast partially or fully. One-day fasts on a consistent basis will strengthen your spirit over time and give you the ability to discipline yourself for longer fasts. Three-day fasts with just water are a powerful way to see breakthroughs. Fasts longer than three days should be done by people with more experience in fasting.

I do not recommend long fasts unless there is an emergency or if one is led by the Holy Spirit to do so. Daniel fasted twenty-one days and saw a great breakthrough for his people (Dan. 9–10). Daniel was also a prophet, and God will use prophets to fast for different reasons to see breakthroughs. Jesus fasted forty days before beginning His ministry. I do know of people who have fasted forty days and have seen great breakthroughs.

A partial fast can include some food such as vegetables and can be done for long lengths. Complete fasts consist of only water, and water is important to cleanse the system of toxins that are released through fasting. The Holy Spirit will reveal to you when you need to fast. A fasted lifestyle is a powerful lifestyle.

WHAT KINDS OF BREAKTHROUGHS CAN YOU EXPECT AS A RESULT OF FASTING?

As a covenant believer being able to live life full of peace and prosperity is part of your salvation package. The enemy fights you for this. This is why we are in a battle. He continues to steal from you what has already been claimed for you. Jesus gave you the authority to stop him from taking your covenant blessings. When you begin to fast and pray for the enemy's hands to be taken off of your stuff, here is what you can expect to see broken off your life.

Fasting will break the spirit of poverty over your life and will prepare the way for prosperity (Joel 2:15, 18–19, 24–26).

The prophet Joel gave the people the proper response to the locust invasion. Locusts represent demons that devour. Locusts represent the spirits of poverty and lack. The locusts had come upon Israel and devoured the harvest. Joel encouraged the people to fast and repent. God promised to hear their prayers and answer by sending corn, wine, and oil.

Corn, wine, and oil represent prosperity, one of the signs of walking in covenant with God. Fasting breaks the spirit of poverty and releases the spirit of prosperity. I have seen countless numbers of believers struggle in the area of their finances. Prosperity is elusive to many. This is because the demons of poverty have not been bound through fasting and prayer.

In Deuteronomy 8:3, 7–9, and 18 God allowed the people to hunger in the wilderness by feeding them with only manna. They ate manna for forty years. This preceded their entering the Promised Land. Fasting helps prepare a believer for the good land. This is a land without scarceness. This is a land with no lack. Fasting humbles the soul (Ps. 35:13). God rewards those who fast (Matt. 6:18). Tremendous blessings are released for those who understand the power of fasting and do it.

Fasting is one of the ways we can break generational strongholds of poverty. Fasting prepares a believer for prosperity by bringing them into a place of humility. God has promised to exalt the humble (1 Pet. 5:6). Financial promotion is part of this exaltation. God gives grace (favor) to the humble (James 4:6). Favor is a part of financial prosperity. Fasting releases grace and favor upon a person's life. This will break the cycle of poverty and failure.

Fasting will break the power of fear that tries to oppress you (Joel 2:21).

Do you desire to see great things happen in your life and in your family? The Lord desires to do great things for His covenant people. Fasting will break the spirit of fear in your life and will prepare the way for great things to happen. These great things include signs and wonders.

Fasting causes you to become more fruitful (Joel 2:22).

Fasting increases the fruit of a believer's life. This includes the fruit of the Spirit. God desires His people to be more fruitful. Fasting helps our ministries, businesses, and careers become more fruitful.

Fasting releases the rain (Joel 2:23).

Rain represents the outpouring of the Holy Spirit. Rain also represents blessing and refreshing. Israel needed the former rain to moisten the ground for planting. They needed the latter rain to bring the crops to maturity. God has promised to give the former and latter rains in response to fasting.

Fasting moistens the ground (the heart) for the planting of the seed (the Word of God). Fasting causes the rain to fall in dry places. If you have not experienced revival in your spirit for a long time, through fasting the Lord can cause the rain of revival to fall in your life so that you can be refreshed and renewed.

Fasting breaks limitations, releases favor, and brings enlargement (Esther 4:14–16).

Fasting was a part of defeating the plans of Haman to destroy the Jews. The whole nation of Israel was delivered because of fasting. Esther needed favor from the king and received it as a result of fasting. Fasting releases favor and brings great deliverance.

The Jews not only defeated their enemies but they were also enlarged. Mordecai was promoted, and Haman was hung. Enlargement comes through fasting. Fasting breaks limitations and gives you more room to expand and grow. God desires to enlarge our borders (Deut. 12:20). God wants us to have more territory. This includes natural and spiritual territory. Fasting breaks limitations and causes expansion.

Fasting will result in answered prayer (Isa. 58:9).

Demonic interference causes many prayers to be hindered. Daniel fasted twenty-one days to break through demonic resistance and receive answers to his prayers. (See Daniel 10.) The prince of Persia withstood the answers for twenty-one days. Daniel's fast helped an angel to break through and bring the answers.

Fasting will cause many answers to prayer to be accelerated. These include prayers for salvation of loved ones and deliverance. Fasting helps to break the frustration of unanswered prayer.

Fasting releases divine guidance (Isa. 58:11).

Many believers have difficulty making correct decisions concerning relationships, finances, and ministry. This causes setbacks and wasted time because of foolish decisions. Fasting will help believers make correct decisions by releasing divine guidance. Fasting eliminates confusion. Fasting causes clarity and releases understanding and wisdom to make correct decisions.

Fasting is recommended for those who are making important decisions such as marriage and ministry/career choices.

Fasting will break generational curses (Isa. 58:12).

Many of the obstacles we face in life are generational. Generational curses result from the iniquity of the fathers. Generational sins such as pride, rebellion, idolatry, witchcraft, occult involvement, Masonry, and lust open the door for evil spirits to operate in families through generations. Demons of destruction, failure, poverty, infirmity, lust, and addiction are major strongholds in the lives of millions of people.

Fasting helps loose the bands of wickedness. Fasting lets the oppressed go free. Fasting helps us to rebuild the old waste places. Fasting reverses the desolation that results from sin and rebellion.

Fasting will cause you to have great victory against overwhelming odds (2 Chron. 20:3).

Jehoshaphat was facing the combined armies of Moab, Ammon, and Edom. He was facing overwhelming odds. Fasting helped him to defeat these enemies. Fasting helps us to have victory in the midst of defeat.

Jehoshaphat called a fast because he was afraid. Fear is another stronghold that many believers have difficulty overcoming. Fasting will break the power of the demon of fear. Spirits of terror, panic, fright, apprehension, and timidity can be overcome through fasting. Freedom from fear is a requirement to live a victorious lifestyle.

Fasting will release the power of the Holy Spirit for the miraculous to occur (Luke 4:14, 18).

Fasting increases the anointing and the power of the Holy Spirit in the life of a believer. Jesus ministered in power after fasting. He healed the sick and cast out devils. All believers are expected to do the same works (John 14:12). Fasting helps us to minister healing and deliverance to our families and others around us. Fasting helps us walk in the power of God. Fasting releases the anointing for miracles to happen in our and our families' lives.

Fasting brings an open reward (Matt. 6:16–18).

God promises rewards to those who fast in secret. It is an open reward. This means that people will see the blessing of God upon your life. Abraham is an example of someone who believed God's promise for a reward.

> After these things the word of the LORD came to Abram in a vision, saying, "Do not be afraid, Abram. I am your shield, your exceedingly great reward."
>
> —Genesis 15:1

Reward is God's favor, abundance, and blessing. Fasting in secret will bring God's reward openly. Fasting will release blessing, abundance, favor, and prosperity. Learn the secret of obtaining God's reward through secret fasting. Everybody doesn't need to know you are fasting. As you are led by the Holy Spirit, make this a private discipline between you and God and see how He rewards you.

> But without faith it is impossible to please Him, for he who comes to God must believe that He is, and that He is a rewarder of those who diligently seek Him.
>
> —Hebrews 11:6

Fasting breaks unbelief and doubt (Matt. 13:58; 17:20).

> Now He did not do many mighty works there because of their unbelief.
>
> —Matthew 13:58

> And Jesus said unto them, Because of your unbelief: for verily I say unto you, If ye have faith as a grain of mustard seed, ye shall say unto this mountain, Remove hence to yonder place; and it shall remove; and nothing shall be impossible unto you.
>
> —Matthew 17:20, kjv

Unbelief is an enemy to operating in the miraculous. Jesus could not operate in the power of God because of the unbelief of the people. The disciples could not cast out a strong demon because of unbelief.

It is important to drive unbelief from your life. And one of the ways this is accomplished is through prayer and fasting. Prayer and fasting helps us clear obstacles to our faith and faith-filled actions.

In the healing revival of 1948–1957 many came into a Healing ministry this way. Franklin Hall wrote a key book, *The Atomic Power With God With Prayer and Fasting.* He called fasting "supercharged prayer." He said the flesh had three primary needs or desires (food, sex, and status) and of these the need for food is dominant. These natural desires are valid, but they can easily become too strong (inordinate desires equal lusts) and dominate us. Thus fasting is the way to assert control on the flesh where it counts.

Fasting, coupled with prayer, is one of the most powerful weapons to breakthrough and overcome unbelief. Jesus preceded His ministry with fasting, and returned in the power of the Spirit into Galilee. Jesus did not struggle with unbelief, and He operated in faith throughout His ministry. When challenged with unbelief in any situation, I encourage you to fast and pray for breakthrough and experience the life and favor God has for you.

PRAYERS AND DECLARATIONS TO RELEASE THE BENEFITS OF FASTING

Lord, I believe in the power of Your chosen fast (Isa. 58).

Lord, let my fasting destroy the yokes that the enemy has set up against me.

Let Your light come into my life through Your chosen fast.

Let health and healing be released to me though Your chosen fast.

Let me see breakthroughs of salvation and deliverance in my life through Your chosen fast.

Let miracles be released in my life through Your chosen fast.

Let Your power and authority be released in my life through Your chosen fast.

I humble my soul through fasting; let Your favor exalt me.

I drive every stubborn demon out of my life through Your chosen fast.

Let Your covenant blessing and mercy be released on me through Your chosen fast.

Nothing is impossible with You, Lord; let my impossibilities become possibilities through Your chosen fast.

Let every assignment of hell against me be broken through Your chosen fast.

Let all pride, rebellion, and witchcraft operating in my life be destroyed through Your chosen fast.

Let Your anointing increase in my life through Your chosen fast.

Let me enjoy restoration through Your chosen fast.

Let all carnality be rebuked from my life through Your chosen fast.

Let all habits and iniquity in me be broken and overcome through Your chosen fast.

Let my prayers be answered speedily through Your chosen fast.

Guide me through Your chosen fast.

Manifest Your glory to me through Your chosen fast.

Let the strongholds of sexual impurity and lust be broken in my life through Your chosen fast.

Let sickness and infirmity be destroyed in my life, and let healing come forth through Your chosen fast.

Let all poverty and lack be destroyed in my life through Your chosen fast.

Remove all oppression and torment from my life through Your chosen fast.

I humble myself with fasting (Ps. 35:13).

I will turn to the Lord with fasting, weeping, and mourning (Joel 2:12).

This "kind" that I face will go out from me through fasting and prayer (Matt. 17:21).

I will fast according the fast chosen by the Lord (Isa. 58:5).

I will proclaim a fast and humble myself before our God, to seek from Him the right way for my family and all our possessions (Ezra 8:21).

I fast to loose the bonds of wickedness, to undo heavy burdens, to the let the oppressed go free, and to break every yoke (Isa. 58:6).

I will set my face toward the Lord God to make requests by prayer and supplication, with fasting, sackcloth, and ashes (Dan. 9:3).

I will fast in the secret place, and my Father sees in secret. He will reward me openly (Matt. 6:18).

I will not depart from the temple of the Lord but will serve God with fastings and prayers night and day (Luke 2:37).

CHAPTER 8
A FUTURE FILLED WITH HOPE

For I know the thoughts that I think toward you, says the LORD,
thoughts of peace and not of evil, to give you a future and a hope.
—JEREMIAH 29:11

GOD HAS GREAT and mighty plans for your life. He established covenant so that He could ensure your success in living out those plans. He has secured your future so that you can live at peace as you grow in your knowledge of Him. He will sustain you and protect you. He will make your way prosperous. Throughout this book I've talked about the keys to living a full and favor-filled life. Part of this is feeling a sense of purpose and knowing you have what you need to live out that purpose. Your purpose is directly linked to your doing what God has created you to do. God has plans for you.

The Bible says in Jeremiah 29:11 that God knows the plans He has for you. He says, "Come to Me, and I will show you great and mighty things." (See Jeremiah 33:3.) Our being able to hear from God comes through Bible study, prayer, and the revealed word of God, or prophecy. His prophetic word brings us hope for our future.

> Remember the word unto thy servant, upon which thou
> hast caused me to hope.
> —PSALM 119:49, KJV

Hopelessness and discouragement will destroy your destiny. Prophecy brings hope and lifts the spirit. I have seen many discouraged believers recharged through the prophetic word. Prophecy reveals the thoughts of God. God's thoughts are peace (shalom). As we have discovered, shalom means blessing, favor, health, success, and prosperity.

God's thoughts are higher (Isa. 55:8–9). We need to hear God's thoughts concerning our lives. God's thoughts will cause you to think higher. God's thoughts will change your life. We can know the mind of the Lord (His plans and purposes). (See Romans 11:34.) God can reveal them to us. Knowing God's plans for your future will help you walk in it.

Here are ten things to help you live up to God's thoughts about your future.

1. HAVE FAITH IN GOD

Without faith it is impossible to please God. Faith is dealing with someone you can't see. A sign or characteristic of a righteous person is faith. They believe God even though they can't see Him. You build faith in God by reading and hearing His Word. The Bible says that faith comes by hearing and hearing by the Word of God.

Those who put their faith in the Lord will dwell in the land and be fed (Ps. 37:3). I don't care how bad the economy gets, if you trust in the Lord, you are not going to starve. It doesn't matter how bad it gets, how many people are losing their jobs, you're going to eat. You are covered by the blood of Jesus. Joblessness, foreclosure, and so on will not be with the righteous. It will not come nigh unto you!

You will not be ashamed in the evil time: and in the days of famine you will be satisfied (Ps. 37:19). When everybody else is hungry, you are sleeping because you ate a good meal. Economy says, "Everybody is hurting." You say, "No! I'm righteous and I will be satisfied. I will not starve. I will not die. I will be satisfied no matter how bad it looks. I am not like everybody else. I am a righteous man. I am a saint of God. I am a child of God. I have a covenant with God. I trust in God. The little that I have is more than the riches of the wicked. I will be satisfied in the day of famine. I can have what I desire because I delight myself in the Lord. The devil is a liar. It is different for me!"

The just shall *live* by faith!

2. Do Not Fret Because of Evildoers

David went through some things. He saw the wicked, especially men like Saul and his own son Absalom who attempted to over throw and take the kingdom. He saw what looked like wicked men prospering, when he—the righteous, the anointed—was hiding out in caves.

He knew he was anointed to be the next king. Samuel told him he was. Samuel poured oil on his head and anointed him to be the next king. But instead of him sitting on the throne, he was hiding in caves and running for his life. And it looked as if the wicked had all the power and success. That's why in the first verse of Psalm 37 he says the one thing you must not allow yourself to do is to fret or get angry when you see things going in a way that doesn't seem right. Don't get upset with wicked people. Don't allow them to disturb your spirit.

You can get messed up looking at other people. You have to keep your heart pure and right. Some of the people you are the kindest to and do the most for can turn their backs on you. When this happens, there is an opportunity for a seed of bitterness to grow.

Bitterness is one of the worst spirits that can get a hold of your life. Bitterness will poison your system; it opens the door for cancer, sickness disease, and all other kinds of problems. That's why you cannot allow the evil that other people do mess you up. Although you cannot control what other people do, you can control what you do, how you respond, and what you allow.

There will always be people out there who don't do right, but you have to keep yourself walking in the love of God and full of the joy of the Lord. Those people may be messed up, but they don't have to mess you up. Fret not because of evildoers!

Psalm 37:3 says, "Trust in the Lord, and do good." Trust that God has everything under control and do good things. Don't allow yourself to do wrong because other people are doing wrong. God is a righteous judge, and His Word says that whatever a man sows that will he also reap (Gal. 6:7). Vengeance is the Lord's; He will repay (Rom. 12:19).

3. Keep Your Heart and Your Mouth

> Keep your heart with all diligence, for out of it spring
> the issues of life.
> —Proverbs 4:23

Your life is affected by what comes out of your heart. What comes out of your heart can always be determined by what comes out of your mouth. From the abundance of the heart the mouth speaks (Matt. 12:34). You can always tell where someone's heart is by what they say.

If you're complaining, whining and criticizing, and speaking negative words all the time, it is because you have not kept your heart clean and pure. You have allowed unforgiveness, bitterness, and anger to get inside of your heart. And that is going to affect your life. Bitter, angry, and critical people always end up in a mess.

4. Delight Yourself in the Lord

"Delight yourself also in the Lord, and He shall give you the desires of your heart" (Ps. 37:4). An easy way to get your desires—just delight yourself in the Lord. They shouldn't be hard. As a believer, you should enjoy the Lord, participating in praise and worship, reading the Word, being in the house of God, and living a saved life. This should not be hard for you if you delight in the Lord. Some people say it is so hard. Which Jesus are you following? The Jesus I know says, "My yoke is easy and my burden is light" (Matt. 11:30). You must be stuck in religion, because when you come to Jesus He makes you walk in green pastures and restores your soul (Ps. 23).

The way of the transgressor is hard.

Delighting yourself in the Lord and His ways is not hard for a believer. It will make manifest the desires of your heart.

5. Bless the Little You Have in Your Hands

> A little that a righteous man hath is better than the
> riches of many wicked.
> —Psalm 37:16, kjv

God can bless a little. In the miracle of the five loaves and two fish, God did more with a few loaves of bread and couple of fish because He blessed it. It fed five thousand.

When you get a little, bless it. It's going to go further than if you had more. God is not limited by how small something is. Start blessing what you have in your hands. Don't try to figure out how it's going to work. There are times when you may have a lot of money and it will just leave your hands if you're not living right.

In 2 Kings 4 there's the story of the widow and the vessels of oil. She had a debt to pay, but all she had was one jar of oil. The prophet Elisha told her go out and borrow empty vessels from all of her neighbors. Upon her return, she shut her door and began to pour the oil from her one jar. And it began to multiply until she had more than enough to sell and repay her debt. God can take the little you have in your hand and bless it. So don't ever be ashamed of a humble start. Bless what you do have and see God multiply it.

6. TAKE RESPONSIBILITY FOR YOUR SUCCESS

> You will make your way prosperous, and then you will
> have good success.
> —JOSHUA 1:8

The responsibility is on you to choose life or death, blessing or cursing. Many times we don't believe our choices are important, and then we don't want responsibility for the things we choose. We want someone else to take responsibility for the choices we make.

You are responsible for making your own way successful and prosperous. You make it successful by meditating on, confessing, living, and applying the Word of God to your life. Your prosperity is not dependent on someone else. Good leaders are important, but your salvation, prosperity, or whatever else doesn't depend on them. It is your responsibility.

We live in a society where people want to blame someone else for where they are. They never want to take responsibility for their own condition. It's always someone else—mother, father, brother, sister, spouse, boss, teacher, enemies, the president. You can prosper through Reagan, Clinton, Bush, or Obama; it doesn't make any difference. God's Word will work when you apply it to your life.

When you're a baby and a child, your parents are responsible for you. But when you become an adult, you are responsible for your own decisions. You can't expect someone to take you by the hand and walk you through life. Here you are forty, fifty, or sixty years old and you're still dealing with the same kinds of issues teenagers are dealing with. It's time to grow up. Paul said that when he became a man, he put away childish things (1 Cor. 13:11).

A successful person, one who knows God's plan for their lives, understands that the freedom they experience in Christ comes with responsibility. They diligently seek after wisdom from God in how to live their lives, and they take responsibility for hearing from God and obeying His instruction, gaining wisdom, learning from their mistakes, rebounding after failure, and staying focused until they see their lives line up with God's plan.

7. Walk in the Power of the Lord

> That at the name of Jesus every knee should bow, of those in heaven, and of those on earth, and of those under the earth, and that every tongue should confess that Jesus Christ is Lord, to the glory of God the Father.
> —Philippians 2:10–11

In Hebrew thought your name represents your character. Many of the names for God are symbolic, illustrative, and figurative. In worship we respond to who God has revealed Himself to be. Knowing the different names of God will help us understand and relate to Him better. When we relate right with God, we also live our lives right.

> And Pharaoh said, "Who is the Lord, that I should obey His voice to let Israel go?"
> —Exodus 5:2

Pharaoh did not know the Lord and asked, "Who is the Lord (Yahweh, Jehovah)?" The Scriptures contain a revelation of the Lord. By reading and confessing these Scriptures, you will have a greater revelation of the greatness and power of the Lord. The Bible describes the Lord's character and mighty acts.

The Hebrew name *Adonai,* or *Adon,* means "lord." The form *Adonai,* used 439 times in the Bible, can be rendered either as "my Lord" or simply as "Lord." The most common name for the Hebrew God (used more than 6,800 times in the Bible) is typically concealed from the modern reader; virtually all standard translations render YHWH as "the Lord" (often printed as "Lord") or "the Eternity."

There is one place in modern English translations where *Yahweh* or YHWH (or, in the KJV, *Jehovah*) is not translated: In Exodus 6:3, in which God reveals His name to Moses: "I am the Lord [YHWH—here it is translated]. I appeared to Abraham, to Isaac, and to Jacob, as God Almighty [El Shaddai], but by My name Lord (Jehovah) I was not known to them" (Exod. 6:2–3). The word translated as "Lord" in the King James Version is *Yahweh* or *Jehovah.*

> I, even I, am the Lord, and besides Me there is no savior.
> —Isaiah 43:11

Jesus is Lord and Savior. The Lord of the Old Testament reveals Himself through Jesus Christ in the New Testament.

> Great is the Lord, and greatly to be praised; and His greatness is unsearchable.
> —Psalm 145:3

> Great is the Lord and most worthy of praise; his greatness no one can fathom.
> —Psalm 145:3, NIV

It is impossible to completely fathom (measure) the greatness of the Lord. Nevertheless, the Lord has given us a glimpse of His greatness, and we can mediate upon Him and wonder at what He has revealed. This will increase our level of fear, obedience, reverence, praise, and worship of the Lord. The Lord is worthy to be praised, and to receive honor, riches, power, dominion, and glory. The Lord is to be feared above all. The Lord is to be loved with all the heart, and we are to cleave to Him. The Lord is greater than all and higher than all. There is no one like the Lord, and no one can be compared to Him. The Lord is holy, merciful, and righteous in all His ways. Let the nations and the people hear and respond with praise, let the whole earth break forth in singing.

The Lord is a healer, restorer, deliverer, savior, protector, defender, promoter, keeper, lover, fighter, creator, and revealer. Allow your faith to increase and receive the many benefits that come from the Lord. And always remember the most important truth, "That if thou shalt confess with thy mouth the Lord Jesus, and shalt believe in thine heart that God hath raised him from the dead, thou shalt be saved" (Rom. 10:9, KJV).

These truths about the Lord will challenge you to come to a higher level of understanding and reverence for the Lord Jesus Christ. They will fill you with power and knowledge and understanding. And these are hardly the beginning of the nature and character of God. Begin to meditate upon them and confess them and watch your revelation and praise go to another level.

8. Recognize God's Provision for the Pattern

When God reveals to us the plan for our lives or the pattern for fulfilling a certain mission or task, we need to know that He will also provide what we need to fulfill the plan. If there is no provision, it may mean that God has not given you that particular task or assignment or it is not yet time to embark upon that phase of the plan. God's provision confirms the plans and patterns He sets before us. Both His pattern and provision must be in place if we are to move forward. God is committed to providing provision for the patterns He gives us.

God gave Moses a pattern to build the tabernacle in the wilderness.

> According to all that I show you, that is, the pattern of
> the tabernacle and the pattern of all its furnishings, just
> so you shall make it.
> —Exodus 25:9

The people gave an offering willingly to provide for this pattern.

> Speak to the children of Israel, that they bring Me an
> offering. From everyone who gives it willingly with his
> heart you shall take My offering.
> —Exodus 25:2

The people were so generous that Moses had to restrain them from giving. The tabernacle was built because God stirred the people to provide.

> And they spoke to Moses, saying, "The people bring
> much more than enough for the service of the work
> which the Lord commanded us to do."
> —Exodus 36:5

As another example, David gave Solomon the pattern of the temple. David received the pattern by the Spirit (1 Chron. 28:19).

A pattern is also a blueprint. There are patterns (plans or blueprints) we can receive by revelation.

> Then David gave his son Solomon the plans for the vestibule, its houses, its treasuries, its upper chambers, its
> inner chambers, and the place of the mercy seat.
> —1 Chronicles 28:11

David not only gave his son Solomon the pattern, but he also gave him provision. David provided gold, silver, and other materials for the building of the temple.

> Moreover, because I have set my affection to the house
> of my God, I have of mine own proper good, of gold and
> silver, which I have given to the house of my God, over
> and above all that I have prepared for the holy house. Even

three thousand talents of gold, of the gold of Ophir, and
seven thousand talents of refined silver, to overlay the
walls of the houses withal: The gold for things of gold, and
the silver for things of silver, and for all manner of work
to be made by the hands of artificers. And who then is
willing to consecrate his service this day unto the LORD?

—1 CHRONICLES 29:3–5, KJV

If a ministry, business, or idea is lacking provision, then maybe
you should review your pattern. Provision follows pattern.

Son of man, describe the temple to the house of Israel,
that they may be ashamed of their iniquities; and let
them measure the pattern.

—EZEKIEL 43:10

It is wise to count the cost before you begin a venture to ensure
success. (See Luke 14:28–30.)

9. EMBRACE THE NEW THINGS

Intelligence is the ability to learn or understand or deal with new or
trying situations. It is the ability to achieve complex goals in complex situations. It is also the ability to solve hard problems. God's
wisdom will give you the intelligence you need to operate in the
"new," although it may seem difficult at first. New things will not
baffle you but challenge you to solve and understand, although it
may seem complex at first.

Being able to adapt to new things is a key to success in an ever-changing world with a God who loves to do new things. Don't be
afraid of change. Ask God for flexibility and humility as He makes
changes in your life and takes you to higher levels in Him. Remember
that His plan is to prosper and give you a future and a hope. In order
to prosper, you have to grow. In order to grow, you have to be challenged and tested.

Behold, the former things have come to pass, and new things I declare; before they spring forth I tell you of them.
—ISAIAH 42:9

Do not call to mind the former things, or ponder things of the past. Behold, I will do something new, now it will spring forth; will you not be aware of it? I will even make a roadway in the wilderness, rivers in the desert.
—ISAIAH 43:18–19

I proclaim to you new things from this time, even hidden things which you have not known. They are created now and not long ago; and before today you have not heard them, so that you will not say, "Behold, I knew them." You have not heard, you have not known.
—ISAIAH 48:6–8

Our Father God is a God of new things! When it comes to paradigms and patterns, the fact of the matter is: humans tend to be much more conservative than God. God is the God of new things! He is forever breaking the molds and casting new ones. In the arena of the establishment of His Kingdom on Earth, He is constantly declaring new things before they spring forth. With the abundance of "Word" and "Faith" teaching the church has been instructed with over the last thirty to forty years, one thing we know quite well is that everything God does, He does by first speaking it, declaring it, proclaiming it! Then, the word that He declares shall not return to Him void without accomplishing the purpose for which it was sent. He always performs what He proclaims.[1]

—STEVEN LAMBERT

Do you want to experience new things from the Lord? One of the keys to experiencing new things is prophecy. The prophetic word releases new things. God speaks new things. God is the God of a new thing, and He desires to do new things in your life. Get involved in a prophetic church, and you will be amazed at the new things that will begin to take place in your life.

10. MEDITATE ON THE WORD

> Blessed is the man that walketh not in the counsel of the ungodly, nor standeth in the way of sinners, nor sitteth in the seat of the scornful. But his delight is in the law of the LORD; and in his law doth he meditate day and night. And he shall be like a tree planted by the rivers of water, that bringeth forth his fruit in his season; his leaf also shall not wither; and whatsoever he doeth shall prosper.
> —PSALM 1:1–3, KJV

The Book of Psalms begins with the value of meditation. Psalm 1 describes the blessed man. The blessed man meditates in the Word day and night. The blessed man prospers in everything.

Everyone wants to be blessed, but few know the secret to being blessed: meditation. Few have the discipline to meditate day and night. Few begin this practice at an early age. It has always been a key to success and prosperity.

Many people struggle to be blessed. Many struggle in life without the blessing of God. Those who learn this key and use it will experience blessing.

Proverbs 10:22 says, "The blessing of the LORD, it maketh rich, and he addeth no sorrow with it" (KJV). The Easy-to-Read Version says it like this: "It is the LORD's blessing that brings wealth, and no hard work can add to it." In other words this is blessing without toil. This is not laboring to be rich, but wealth without toil and stress. You do not have to kill yourself to be blessed.

The blessed man of Psalm 1 meditates in the Word day and night. Meditation is a sure path to prosperity and success. Whatever this man does will prosper.

In Joshua 1:8 we find the only place the word *success* is found in the King James Version of the Bible.

> This book of the law shall not depart out of thy mouth; but thou shalt meditate therein day and night, that thou mayest observe to do according to all that is written therein: for then thou shalt make thy way prosperous, and then thou shalt have good success.

Success is the Hebrew word *sakal* meaning to be prudent, be circumspect, to act wisely, to understand, to prosper, give attention to, consider, ponder, be prudent, to have insight, have comprehension, to act circumspectly, act prudently.

We can see from this verse that meditation is connected to wisdom. Meditation will help you access the wisdom of God. The key to success is wisdom as we discovered in chapter 4. Wisdom is one of the greatest benefits of meditating in the Word of God. Getting wisdom is the most important thing you can do. Whatever else you get, get insight. Wisdom is best, wisdom is supreme. Wisdom is the first and primary thing you need to succeed in life. (See Proverbs 4:7.)

> Happy is the man that findeth wisdom, and the man that getteth understanding. For the merchandise of it is better than the merchandise of silver, and the gain thereof than fine gold. She is more precious than rubies: and all the things thou canst desire are not to be compared unto her. Length of days is in her right hand; and in her left hand riches and honour. Her ways are ways of pleasantness, and all her paths are peace. She is a tree of life to them that lay hold upon her: and happy is every one that retaineth her.
>
> —PROVERBS 3:13–18, KJV

These verses emphasize the value of wisdom. It is more precious than rubies. Nothing compares to wisdom. Wisdom results in long life. Wisdom brings you to riches and honor. Wisdom leads to peace.

Wisdom promotes happiness. This is also what biblical meditation will produce in your life.

> Riches and honour are with me; yea, durable riches and righteousness. My fruit is better than gold, yea, than fine gold; and my revenue than choice silver. I lead in the way of righteousness, in the midst of the paths of judgment: That I may cause those that love me to inherit substance; and I will fill their treasures.
>
> —PROVERBS 8:18–21, KJV

Wisdom produces riches and honor. Wisdom will cause you to inherit substance. Wisdom will fill your treasures. When you find wisdom, you will find life. You will obtain the favor of the Lord (Prov. 8:35). Meditation in the Word uncovers and releases God's wisdom.

FAITH DECLARATIONS

Because of Christ, I am free. Whom the Son sets free is free indeed (John 8:36).

I do not put my trust in man. I do not put my trust in flesh. I put my trust in God (Ps. 56:4).

I live by faith. I walk by faith and not by sight (2 Cor. 5:7).

I am responsible for my decisions and my choices. I make a decision. I choose life. I choose blessings. I choose the Word of God. I choose wisdom.

I thank you, Lord, that I am responsible for making my own way prosperous and having good success.

I have faith to speak to mountains, and they will obey me (Mark 11:23).

My heart will never depart from You. I will always serve God.

Thank You, Lord, for prosperity. I will flourish because I live in the days of the Messiah.

I will have prosperity, and I will have good success because of God's grace in Jesus's name.

Prayers to Activate the New Things of God

Lord, I declare that the former things have come to pass. Now I receive the new things that will spring forth (Isa. 42:9).

I will not call to my mind the former things, or ponder the things of the past. I look to the new things that the Lord will do. They will spring forth now (Isa. 43:18–19).

I receive new things from this time and not what was created long along. I receive even hidden things I have not known (Isa. 48:6–8).

I am a new creature in Christ. Old things have passed away. All things have become new (2 Cor. 5:17).

I will sing a new song unto the Lord for He has done marvelous things (Ps. 98:1).

Behold, You make all things new (Rev. 21:5).

Lord, bring new things to me out of your treasures (Matt. 13:52).

Lord, put new wine in new bottles for me that both may be preserved (Luke 5:38).

Your mercies to me are new every morning. Great is Your faithfulness (Lam. 3:23).

I look for new heavens and a new earth that You have promised (2 Pet. 3:13).

Lord, put within me a new heart and a new spirit. Take away my stony heart and give me a heart of flesh (Ezek. 36:26).

Let my barns be filled with plenty, and my presses burst out with new wine (Prov. 3:10).

I put on the new man, which is created after God in righteousness and true holiness (Eph. 4:24).

I purge out the old leaven that I may be a new lump (1 Cor. 5:7).

By a new and living way, I draw near to God with a true heart in full assurance of faith (Heb. 10:20–22).

Lord, write for me a new commandment, because the darkness is past and true light now shines (1 John 2:8).

CONFESSIONS FOR MEDITATING ON THE WORD

I will meditate also of all the Lord's work and talk of His doings (Ps. 77:12).

I will meditate on the Lord's precepts and contemplate His ways (Ps. 119:15).

Princes also did sit and speak against me, but I meditate on the Lord's statutes (Ps. 119:23).

Let the proud be ashamed; for they dealt perversely with me without a cause, but I will meditate on thy precepts (Ps. 119:78).

My eyes are awake during the night watches that I may meditate on the Lord's Word (Ps. 119:148).

I remember the days of old; I meditate on all thy works; I muse on the work of thy hands (Ps. 143:5).

I meditate upon these things; give myself wholly to them; that my profiting may appear to all (1 Tim. 4:15).

I love the law of the Lord; it is my meditation all the day (Ps. 119:97).

The law of the Lord is my delight, and in His law I meditate day and night (Ps. 1:2).

I shall be made to understand the way of the Lord's precepts, so I shall meditate on His wonderful works (Ps. 119:27).

I will lift my hands up to the Lord's commandments, which I love, and will meditate on His statutes (Ps. 119:48).

A book of remembrance will be written for me, who fears the Lord and meditates on His name (Mal. 3:16).

I will meditate on the Book of the Law day and night (Josh. 1:8).

NOTES

CHAPTER 1
COVENANT WITH GOD GUARANTEES LIFE AND FAVOR

1. J. E. Leonard, *I Will Be Their God*, (Hamilton, Illinois: Laudemont Press, 1992). 6.
2. James W. Goll, *Deliverance From Darkness* (Grand Rapids, MI: Chosen, 2010), 168–169.
3. Ibid., 168.
4. The Elijah List, "James Goll on 'Generational Blessings,'" http://www.elijahlist.com/words/display_word/3213 (accessed February 10, 2015).
5. Ibid.

CHAPTER 3
TAPPING INTO THE FAVOR OF GOD

1. Biblestudytools.com, s.v. "charis," http://www.biblestudytools.com/lexicons/greek/kjv/charis.html (accessed February 10, 2015).
2. Ibid.

CHAPTER 4
A LIFE OF EXCELLENCE AND WISDOM

1. Richard Ostella, "The Excellence of Christian Love (1 Cor. 12:31-13:3)," Bible.org. June 9, 2009, https://bible.org/seriespage/excellence-christian-love-1-cor-1231-133 (accessed December 15, 2014).
2. Welcome to Kids Answers, "God Speaks of the Ant in His Word, the Bible," March 23, 2010, http://www.answersingenesis.org/articles/ka/v5/n2/ant-in-bible (accessed December 15, 2014).
3. John Johnston, "The Foresight and Diligence of the Ant," Biblehub.com, http://biblehub.com/sermons/auth/johnston/the_foresight_and_diligence_of_the_ant.htm (accessed December 19, 2014).

CHAPTER 6
THIEVES THAT COME TO KILL AND DESTROY A GOOD LIFE

1. Jean Calvin, *Institutes of the Christian Religion Volume 1* (n.p.: Hardpress, 2013), 296.

CHAPTER 8
A FUTURE FILLED WITH HOPE

1. Steven Lambert, "Now I Declare New Things!", SLM.org, www .slm.org/prophetc/articles/new_things.pdf (accessed February 10, 2015).